THE ATLANTIC CRITICAL STUDIES

WILLIAM SHAKESPEARE'S *Hamlet*

RATRI RAY

ATLANTIC
PUBLISHERS & DISTRIBUTORS (P) LTD

Published by

ATLANTIC

PUBLISHERS & DISTRIBUTORS (P) LTD

7/22, Ansari Road, Darya Ganj,
New Delhi-110002
Phones : +91-11-40775252, 23273880, 23275880, 23280451
Fax : +91-11-23285873
Web : www.atlanticbooks.com
E-mail : orders@atlanticbooks.com

Branch Office
5, Nallathambi Street, Wallajah Road,
Chennai-600002
Phones : +91-44-64611085, 32413319
E-mail : chennai@atlanticbooks.com

Printed in India at Nice Printing Press, A-33/3A, Site-IV, Industrial Area, Sahibabad, Ghaziabad, U.P.

General Preface

The Atlantic Critical Studies are study-aids modeled on the study-aids available in England and America, among other places, and are primarily meant for the students of English literature in Indian universities.

However, in consideration of the local conditions and the various constraints under which our students have to study—non-availability of relevant critical books, dearth of foreign and Indian journals, inaccessibility to good, well-equipped libraries, just to mention a few of them—the models have been considerably improved upon, both qualitatively and quantitatively.

Thus, while these Studies are meant to be comprehensive and self-sufficient, the distinguished scholars who have prepared these study materials, have taken special care to combine lucidity and profundity in their treatment of the texts.

The select bibliography at the end is meant not only to acknowledge the sources used but also to help a student in the pursuit of further studies if he/she wants to.

Atlantic believes in quality and excellence. These studies will only reconfirm it.

MOHIT K. RAY
Chief Editor [English Literature]
Atlantic Publishers & Distributors (P) Ltd.
New Delhi

Introduction

Shakespeare, like Sir Walter Raleigh and Sir Philip Sidney, has come to embody the very spirit of Elizabethan-Jacobean England. He is not, however, limited within this narrow sphere, for he is a universal figure. His greatness as a literary figure did not go unrecognized in his own time, for Ben Jonson, one of his great contemporaries had said that he loved him "this side idolatry". His great creative imagination did not isolate him from everyday life. Indeed, he had a strong down-to-earth approach to the practical aspects of day-to-day life, which brought him material prosperity, so that he died as one of the richest men of his village. By the time he bade farewell to the stage, he had come to partially own the theatrical company that staged his plays, had raised his family to the status of landed gentry with its own coat-of-arms and had bought the most valuable property in his village. These achievements belie the popular concepts of a genius as a neglected, impoverished and impractical being.

Such achievements are more than enough for an ordinary man, yet they are practically nothing when we confront Shakespeare the dramatist. He stands unrivalled—whether as a dramatist, a poet, or a sonneteer. Within the two decades that belong to his period of artistic productivity, he poured out a continuous stream of poems, sonnets and plays, that has hardly been equalled before or since. There were many rules and conventions laid down for poets and dramatists. Sometimes, he followed them and at other times, confident of the power of his inborn talent, he disregarded them. As shall be seen in the ensuing chapters, different elements of the play, e.g. the plot, characterization, style, etc. had all reached such harmonious excellence in his plays that they have not only stood the test of time, but also provided material for emulation and speculation. Different schools of criticism, whether Greek or European or Indian, cannot exhaust his infinite variety. Arnold had indeed expressed his nature when he had said that we can question others, Shakespeare is beyond all questions.

Concentrating only on his dramatic works, we find a startling variety in this field. He was alone in his time in writing plays of many different kinds—tragedies, comedies and histories. Marlowe wrote only tragedies (and that, too, of one kind only), Ben Jonson wrote satirical comedies and served to highlight Shakespeare's versatility. Within these three genres of plays, Shakespeare showed great variety. Taking up tragedy only, all four of the prevailing types are to be found in him. *Macbeth* is a conqueror tragedy, *Othello* a villain tragedy, *Romeo and Juliet* a domestic tragedy and *Hamlet*, the play under discussion, exemplifies that highly popular contemporary mode, a revenge tragedy; yet these labels are but superficial tags, utterly unable to express the complexity and richness of his plays.

Apart from these four categories mentioned above, another categorization, based on chronology, has been made of his tragedies. It has to be remembered that these labels are made only as a matter of convenience for the scholar and the student.

They are:

The Early Tragedies: *Titus Andronicus*, *Romeo and Juliet*.

The Great Tragedies: *Hamlet*, *Othello*, *King Lear*, *Macbeth*.

> The Roman Tragedies: *Julius Caesar*, *Antony and Cleopatra*, *Coriolanus*.

In his tragedies as well as comedies, Shakespeare goes down to the very springs of life, down to its mysterious depths. As Una Ellis-Fermor has put it in *The Jacobean Drama*:

> Always, from the shaping of the whole play down to details of imagery, there is, in Shakespeare's treatment, what seems an instinctive knowledge of the roots of being from which phenomena spring.[1]

NOTE

1. Una Ellis-Fermor; *The Jacobean Drama*, London, Methuen, University Paperbacks, p. 248.

Contents

1

The Background

(a) The Socio-political Background

No individual, or his work, can be separated from his background and it is very necessary that the socio-political background of a writer be taken into account when a study of his work is undertaken. Some of the relevant socio-political events of Shakespeare's time are given below in chronological order, which shall be followed by some more detailed account. Religion was one of the chiefest preoccupations of the day and consequently, the main religious events are mentioned as well as the scientific inventions. Queen Elizabeth's time was one of great geographical expansion as well as military exploits and these too are mentioned below.

A chronological table

1558 — Queen Mary I dies. Elizabeth I succeeds.

— Mary Queen of Scots marries the French Dauphin. The French capture Calais.

'59 — Mary Queen of Scots declares herself the Queen of England.

— War between Spain and France ends.

— Church of England re-established more firmly.

'60 — The Scottish Parliament establishes the Reformed Church and breaks with Rome.

'61 — Mary Queen of Scots returns from France. She clashes with the Calvinists.

'62 — The Huguenots begin emigrating from France to England.

'63 — Bubonic plague in Europe.

'64 — Shakespeare born. Anglo-French war ends. England at war with Spain. Galileo born.

— The Thirty-Nine Articles adopted by the Church of England. Queen Elizabeth tries to enforce unity of religion.

'67 — Mary Queen of Scots abdicates. Rugby Chapel founded.

'68 — Mary Queen of Scots flees to England. She is held captive by Queen Elizabeth.

'69 — Rebellion of Roman Catholic earls crushed.

'70 — Pope Pius V excommunicates Queen Elizabeth.

'74 — Burbage gets licence to build the first permanent theatre in London.

'76 — Tycho Brahe begins his astronomical observations. Fifth French Religious war ends.

— Burbage opens the first theatre of England at Shoreditch, in London.

'77 — England makes treaty with the Dutch.

— Sir Francis Drake begins circumnavigation of the globe in the Pelican.

'80 — Sir Francis Drake completes circumnavigation.

'81 — Conversion to Roman Catholicism declared to be treason in England.

— Galileo discovers the law of the pendulum.

'83 — Plot against the queen.

— Humphrey Gilbert takes possession of Newfoundland for England.

'84 — Sir Walter Raleigh discovers, names and starts to colonize Virginia.

'86 — England wins the battle of Zutphen in which Sir Philip Sidney dies.

— Plot against the Queen. Mary Queen of Scots implicated and convicted of treason.

— Thomas Cavendish begins the third circumnavigation of the globe.

'87 — Rose Theatre built by Henslowe.

— Mary Queen of Scots executed for treason.

'88 — Defeat of the Spanish Armada by Sir Francis Drake.

'89 — Galileo publishes the results of his experiments with falling bodies.

'92 — John Davis discovers Falkland Islands.

'93 — Absence from the church on Sundays made punishable by law.

'95 — Southwell the mystical poet is executed for celebrating Mass.

'96 — England, France and Netherlands form alliance against Spain.

— Peasant Revolt in Oxfordshire.

'97 — Second Spanish Armada sent against England is destroyed by a storm.

— Statutory provision for Poor Relief. Beggary made illegal. Transporting of convicts to colonies.

'98 — The Bodleian Library begun. Globe Theatre opened.

1601 — Earl of Essex raises rebellion against the Queen and is executed.

'02 — The East India Company dispatches its first trading fleet to Sumatra.

'03 — Queen Elizabeth dies. Accession of James VI of Scotland as James I England.

'04 — Peace with Spain.

— Banishment of Roman Catholic priests provokes Gunpowder plot to blow up parliament houses.

— Acts against priests and recusants. Anglican canons made.

— Silk manufacture begins in England.

’05 — Gunpowder plot discovered. Conspirator Guy Fawkes arrested. English colonists land in Barbados.

’07 — First permanent settlement Jamestown is founded on American mainland.

’08 — Failure of plan for union with Scotland.

— Invention of the microscope and telescope in Netherlands.

’10 — Judicial decision against royal proclamations.

— Explorer Hudson sails through Hudson Bay.

’11 — Parliament dissolved.

— Land granted in Northern Ireland to Scottish and English protestants.

’12 — Alliance with German protestant princes.

— Witches hanged at Lancashire, the last recorded executions for heresy.

’13 — Princess Elizabeth marries Elector Frederick V.

— Galileo publishes his acceptance of Copernican theory.

’16 — Shakespeare dies. Sir Walter Raleigh sets forth in search of El Dorado.

It can be seen how precarious the position of Queen Elizabeth was when Shakespeare was born. Plots against her were being continually hatched at home, and there was continuous warfare with the nations abroad. It took Queen Elizabeth quite a few years to settle firmly on the throne. Mary Queen of Scots was a continual source of trouble and finally when after plotting against the Queen who was, after all, her cousin, she met with the fate proper for a traitor, Queen Elizabeth was more or less secure on the throne. She was a very fine stateswoman and a good sovereign—patriotic as well as courageous. She was tolerant in her religious policies and put an end to religious controversies. G.M. Trevelyan points this out:

> In the year in which the Queen succeeded her sister Mary, Puritanism was mainly a foreign doctrine imported from Geneva and Rhineland, when she died it was rootedly and characteristically English.[1]

Her long reign, peaceful and prosperous, helped the spirit of Anglicanism drive deep roots in the country. Again, as the same writer points out:

> At the end of her reign, it had become a real religion; its services were dear to many, after more than forty years of use in the ancient churches of England.[2]

Just as there were problems of succession in the beginning of Elizabeth's reign (Mary Queen of Scots being a strong claimant), so were there problems and speculations towards the end of her reign. This was inevitable, as she left no direct or obvious heir to the throne. But during the decades of her reign, she gave security and prosperity to her country by her wisdom and moderation.

An important feature of the time was its continuous growth and expansion. The structure of society fostered this spirit. There were class barriers, but these were accepted, not resented. So there were no frictions between the classes to hamper any kind of growth. There were the feudal lords and the working classes, but no oppression of the latter by the former. It was the freedom of opportunity for everyone that mattered, not equality. The kind of difference between the lord of the manor and the peasantry that existed in medieval England did not exist in Elizabethan England:

> In Tudor England, such rigid lines were rendered impossible by the number and variety of men in intermediate classes and occupations, who were closely connected, in the business and amusement of daily life, with those above and those below them in social status.... Such was the England known and approved by Shakespeare.[3]

The dignity of labour was no mere theory but a proven fact. Everyone earned a fair wage for work that was done honestly and efficiently. This helped a spirit of self-reliance and self-respect grow in the mind of ordinary people.

Most of the people were responsible self-respecting members of society and as such felt responsible towards the poor and the disabled. So the Poor Law was passed for the relief of the unfortunate. The system of Justice of Peace was instituted in which influential and responsible persons were made to minister justice in minor cases. These Justices of Peace or JPs were, in their turn, controlled by the Privy Council, a higher organization.

By this time, the economical side of society also received boost as the factory system was started. This brought about industrial prosperity. Mining improved to such an extent that many metals like lead, copper, iron and tin, which had been scarce, became available to all. Coal became cheaper, so homes became warmer. Glass window-panes became available so homes became brighter and lighter.

The great explorer Sir Francis Drake brought national glory by his two important achievements, the circumnavigation of the globe and the defeat of the Spanish Armada. The latter was a landmark achievement, for it put an end to threats from the sea. A few years later, a second Armada was sent, but it perished in a storm. This acted as a national confirmation of the faith that the English were the favoured people of the gods. These were, from every point of view, the days of prosperity, security and also of expansion, G.M. Trevelyan sums up:

> By the end of Elizabethan's reign, not only was English commerce and finance thus revising and expanding on a modern basis, but her ancient rivals were in rapid decline.[4]

This expansion and prosperity continued during the Jacobean Age as well. London continued to grow (it was only one square mile in area when Shakespeare arrived there) and industry flourished. One such example has been given above—silk started being manufactured in England. Not many significant changes took place during the next forty years, for those changes that did take place were political ones, not agricultural or industrial changes. When King James VI of Scotland who was a distant cousin of Queen Elizabeth, acceeded to the throne of England as King James I of England, it brought about a union of the royal families of England and Scotland. The two kingdoms remained obstinately separated though the King tried very hard to bring them together. Culturally also, Scotland, though much nearer than Holland, was not so influential as the latter.

In the very first year of his reign, King James made peace with Spain, thus removing all obstacles for maritime trade. Once the seas were safe, colonization started with great vigour. Settlers from England started moving to the fabled lands of new England, Virginia, etc. The seeds of the British empire were sown even as the Holy Roman Empire was declining. Emigrations were organized by the Virginia company and the Massachusetts Bay Company. These pioneers were motivated by religious as well as commercial motives. Such events interest the historian. Posterity remembers one name—Shakespeare:

> His works could never have been produced in any other period than those late Elizabethan and early Jacobean times in which it was his luck to live.[5]

(b) The Literary Background

Just as, in Italy, the spirit of the Renaissance manifested itself through painting and sculpture it found its expression in England through literature. A host of gifted poets and dramatists (as well as prose-writers) were living and writing at this time. Shakespeare's work was strongly rooted in fertile soil. A chronological table is given below which takes in the main literary events of the time, the birth and death of prominent literary figures. Some influential works of the continent have also been mentioned. It is not possible to include the numerous works that were being written, published and staged during this fruitful time. Only a few have been mentioned. The table begins with the first performance of *Ralph Roister Doister*, the year before our poet's birth. Shakespeare's own works are not mentioned as they will be dealt with in the right context (vide ch. 3 *infra*).

A chronological table

1554 — Sir Philip Sidney and Lyly born. *Ralph Roister Doister* staged. Bandello's stories published.

'57 — Tottel's *Miscellany*. Cavendish completes the biography of Thomas Wolsey.

’58 — Kyd, Greene, Peele, Lodge born.

’61 — *Gorboduc* performed. Bacon born. Castiglione’s *The Courtier.*

’63 — Drayton and Donne born. Foxe’s *Book of Martyrs.*

’64 — Shakespeare and Marlowe and Galileo born.

’66 — Gascoigne’s *Supposes.* Painter’s *Palace of Pleasure,* Vol. I.

’67 — Campion and Nashe born. *Palace of Pleasure,* Vol. II.

’70 — Roger Ascham’s *The Schoolmaster.*

’72 — Camoens (Spain) *Os Lusiados.* Donne born.

’73 — Tasso’s (Italian) *Aminta.*

’75 — Heywood and Tourneur born.

— *Appius and Viginia, Gammer Gurton’s Needle.* Fleming’s translation of Virgil’s *Bucolics, Georgics.*

’76 — *The Paradise of Dainty Devises.*

’77 — Holinshed’s *Chronicles.* Translation of Ovid, *Epistolae Heroidum.*

’78 — Lyly’s *Euphues.*

’79 — Spenser’s *Shepherd’s Calendar.* Lord North’s translation of Plutarch’s *Lives.* Gosson’s *School of Abuse.*

’80 — Montaigne’s (French) *Essais,* Bks. I & II.

’82 — Hakluyts’ *Voyages.*

’85 — Kyd’s *Spanish Tragedy.*

’86 — Sir Philip Sidney dies. Lyly’s *Endimion.*

’87 — *Tamburlaine,* Lyly’s *Gallathea. The Misfortunes of Arthur.* Monteverdi’s (Italian) *Madrigals,* Bk I.

’89 — *Jew of Malta* by Marlowe. Puttenham’s *Arte of English Poesie.*

’90 — *Faerie Queene,* Bks, I-III published. Lodge’s *Rosalynde.*

'91 — Sidney's *Astrophel and Stella*, Peele's *Old Wives' Tale*, Marlowe's *Edward II*.

— Sir John Harington's translation of Ariosto's *Orlando Furioso* at the Queen's command.

'92 — Revised *Arcadia*. Daniel's *To Delia* (sonnets), Marlowe's *Hero and Leander*. *Arden of Feversham* (Anon.)

1595 — Spenser's *Amoretti* (Sonnet-sequence), Sidney's *Apology for Poetry*.

'98 — Francis Meres' *Palladis Tamia*.

'99 — Spenser dies. Davies's *Nosce Teipsum*.

'1600 — *England's Helicon*, *England's Parnassus*, Jonson's *Cynthia's Revels*, Dekker's *Shoemaker's Holiday*.

'01 — Dekker and Marston's *Satiromastix*, Jonson's *Poetaster*, Marston's *What You Will*.

'03 — Dowland's *Third Book of Songs*, Heywood's *A Woman Killed with Kindness*, Jonson's *Sejanus*, Marston's *The Dutch Courtezan*.

'04 — Chapman's *Bussy D'Ambois*, Marston's *The Malcontent*.

'05 — Drayton's *Collected Poems*, Bacon's *Advancement of Learning*, collaborated play *Eastward Ho!*, Middleton's *A Trick to Catch the Old One*.

'06 — Lyly dies, *Yorkshire Tragedy* (Anon.), Jonson's *Volpone*, Tourneur's *The Revenger's Tragedy*.

'07 — Beaumont and Fletcher's *Knight of the Burning Pestle*.

'08 — Fuller and Milton born. Fletcher's *The Faithful Shepherdess*. Chapman's *Duke of Byron*.

'09 — Beaumont and Fletcher's *Philaster*, Fulke Gereville's *Mustapha*, Tourneur's *Atheist's Tragedy*.

'10 — Donne's *Pseudo-Martyr*. Jonson's *The Alchemist*.

'11 — Spenser's *Collected Works*, *The Authorised Version of the Bible*. *A King and No King*.

'12 — Crashaw born. Chapman's *Iliad* I-XXIV, Donne's *Second Annivarsarie*, Drayton's *Poly-Olbion*, Webster's *The White Devil.*

'13 — Constable and Overbury die. Purchas's *Pilgrimage.*

'14 — Overbury's *Characters.* Lodge's *Works of Seneca.*

'15 — Sir Walter Raleigh's *History of the World*, Jonson's *Bartholomew Fair.* Webster's *The Duchess of Malfi.*

'16 — Shakespeare dies. Jonson given royal pension. Chapman's *Whole Works of Homer.* Jonson's *Works.*

As this table shows, the few years from Sidney's birth in 1554 to Shakespeare's death in 1616 cover the best time of literary efflorescence in England. The most familiar names of the Elizabethan and Jacobean times come later than Sidney. The Tudor dynasty had a rose as the emblem and if the literature of the Renaissance is compared with a rose, then it can be said that what Sidney saw in his lifetime was only a bud which later opened out to spread out in unequalled beauty and fragrance.

Drama, the glory of the Elizabethan and Jacobean era, had barely started in Sidney's time. The plays that were being written and performed were as nothing to those that Shakespeare and others were to write, but it cannot be denied that they prepared the ground for the followers. It is not surprising that Sidney condemned contemporary drama, except for *Gorboduc* which he praised:

> Our tragedies and comedies not without cause cried out against, observing rules neither of honest civility nor of skilful poetry: excepting Gorboduc (again I say of those that I have seen,) which notwithstanding as it is full of stately speeches and well-sounding phrases, climbing to the height of Seneca's style, and as full of notable morality, which it doth most delightfully teach, and so obtain the very end of poesy.[6]

Gorboduc, today, has more of a historical interest than as a work of literary merit. Sidney praised it because there was nothing superior to it. *Ralph Roister Doister*, a rollicking comedy, had been staged ten years before Shakespeare's birth. *The Misfortunes of Arthur*, a play in the nature of a history, had been written for the Queen's entertainment in 1587. These works have only historical importance today and cannot by any means be considered seriously as works of great merit.

The prospect is little better than drama when we turn to narrative poetry, songs and sonnets, all of which Shakespeare wrote. Spenser's *Shepherds Calendar* and parts of *Faerie Queen* had been published before Shakespeare's own narrative poems. Tottel had published his famous *Miscellany* which included the sonnets of Wyatt and Surrey. The famous sequences of Elizabethan love-sonnet started being written by the end of the sixteenth century, reaching their climax in Shakespeare's sequence. The most flourishing genre was that of the lyric. The best lyrics were written by the "Elizabethan nest of singing-birds" from 1580 to 1620, and were being collected and published. Shakespeare's plays are full of songs and, in writing them, he took the help of collections, adapting the words to suit his own requirements. These were mostly light-hearted love-songs:

> The songs-lyric, as developed in accord with the musical art of the time, is too light an instrument to utter the deeper notes of passion and its theme is fanciful love.[7]

As the Elizabethan Age advanced, the output became more and more prolific as well as dazzling. Lyric poetry, narrative poetry, discursive poetry—all flourished in a manner hardly equalled before or since. Prose, which is of minor importance to us (only as the sources of Shakespeare's plays) was developed not only in the romances of Sidney, Lyly and others, but also in the philosophical works of writers like Bacon, Hooker, Sir Thomas Browne *et al.*

It is drama which is the most important of the literacy genres for our present purposes. The University Wits took London by storm by starting with Kyd's *The Spanish Tragedy*, a revenge tragedy. Marlowe's very first attempt *Tamburlaine* (a conqueror tragedy) became so popular that he quickly wrote the second part of the play. As theatres were established by Burbage and Henslowe, plays were in great demand. The dramatists had ample opportunity for experimenting with different kinds of plays and finding the form that suited them. Shakespeare was specially versatile and no one could rival him in the range of his plays or otherwise, but each of the playwrights could find and settle down with the form that suited them the best, as Ben Jonson did with his humour comedies and Beaumont and Fletcher with their tragi-comedies.

The dramatists were highly influenced by classical writers. Seneca for example, was a prevailing influence. Kyd set the example:

> It was the genius of Thomas Kyd that seized upon the essential effects of Senecan action and adapted them, with much relaxation of rules, to the conditions of the public stage.[8]

F.T. Bowers has categorized these tragedies, known as the Blood-and-thunder tragedies, into four divisions: Conqueror tragedy (*Tamburlaine*, *Macbeth*, etc.), Revenge tragedy (*The Spanish Tragedy*, *Hamlet*, etc.), Villain tragedy (*The Changeling*, *Othello*, etc.), and Domestic tragedy (*A Women Killed With Kindness*, *Romeo and Juliet*, etc.) There are many tragedies that cannot be contained within just one group. Webster's *The Duchess of Malfi* for example, is a revenge tragedy as well as a domestic tragedy. Shakespeare's *Othello* is a villain tragedy as well as a domestic tragedy.

Comedy too, flourished in the hands of Lyly, Peele, Greene, Shakespeare, Ben Jonson and others. M.C. Bradbrook has divided Elizabethan society into three categories, the Court, the Country and the City, and ascribes different kinds of comedy to each. The comedies of Shakespeare come mostly under the first of these, and those of Ben Jonson under the third. There is great variety within this kind of play. There are Romantic comedies like those written by Shakespeare, Satirical comedies like those of Ben Jonson, Problem comedies like the four written by Shakespeare, Tragi-comedies like those by Beaumont and Fletcher, and Romances like the last plays of Shakespeare.

Numerous masques were also used for courtly entertainment. Those of Ben Jonson were specially successful. Shakespeare used the device quite frequently in his plays.

Shakespeare's works, thus were firmly rooted into the soil of Elizabethan England and he is the ideal product of his milieu. Another poet, four centuries later, points out the relevance of the background:

> No poet, no artist of any art, has his complete meaning alone. His significance, his appreciation is the appreciation of his relation to the dead poets and artists.[9]

NOTES

1. G.M. Trevelyan, *Illustrated English Social History*, Vol. 2, Harmondswerth: Penguin Book Ltd., 1964, p. 86.
2. *Ibid.*
3. *Ibid.*, p. 62.
4. *Ibid.*, p. 123.
5. *Ibid.*, p. 125.
6. D.J. Enright, and Ernst de Chickera (eds.), *English Critical Texts: 16th Century to 20th Century*, Oxford: Oxford University Press, 2002, p. 40.
7. Frederict Ives Carpenter, *English Lyric Poetry: 1500-1700*. London: Blackie and Son Ltd., No. date, p. 47.
8. Hardin Craig, *The Literature of the English Renaissance: 1485-1660*, New York: Collier Books, 1862, p. 80.
9. T.S. Eliot, *Three Essays*, Calcutta: Oxford University Press, 1979, p. 17.

2

Life and Works

(a) A Short Biography

Many biographies of Shakespeare have been written but it cannot be denied that a lot of the details supplied therein are not very dependable. Anecdotes about him abound, but they are more legendary than historical, particularly those about his early life. Details about his later life, especially from the time that his group became accepted at Court, are historically true and fully reliable. As usually happens, in the case of well-known figures, Shakespeare also became invested with an aura of glory, all the more pronounced as this renown was not posthumous but attained during his lifetime. In the seventeenth century, Fuller wrote a brief biography in his famous *Worthies* (1662) and John Aubrey in his *Lives of Eminent Men*. The first modern editor of Shakespeare, Nicholas Rowe, took material from many other sources as well in the biography given in his edition of the plays. More intensive research has been done by modern biographers. It has to be acknowledged, however, that more material is available on Shakespeare than on his other contemporaries. A chronological table of the important events of his life is given below:

A chronological table of the chief events of his life

1564 — Apr. 23, the supposed date of birth of Shakespeare.

— Apr. 26, Shakespeare was christened at the local parish church of Stratford-upon-Avon.

'71 — Possible time of enrolment in the local school.

'78 — His father's fortunes undergo reverses and he is, possibly, withdrawn from school at this time, or perhaps later.

'82 — Shakespeare gets married to Anne Hathaway.

'83 — Birth of Susanna, his first child.

'85 — The twins, Hamnet and Judith, were born.

'86 — Shakespeare's supposed departure for London.

'93 — *Venus and Adonis* published by Richard Field.

'94 — *Rape of Lucrece* pub. *Titus Andronicus* staged. *The Taming of the Shrew*.[1]

'95 — *A Midsummer Night's Dream*.

'96 — Death of Hamnet his only son. *Sonnets*.

'97 — Shakespeare buys New Place. *The Merchant of Venice*.

'99 — He buys shares in the Globe Theatre. *Much Ado*, *As You Like It*, *Twelfth Night*, *Henry V*, *Julius Caesar*.

1602 — The birth of his first grand child. He buys one hundred and seven acres of land. *All's Well that Ends Well*, *Troilus and Cressida*, *Hamlet*.

'04 — His company taken under royal patronage and given the name of the King's Men. *Measure for Measure*, *Othello*.

'05 — *Macbeth*.

'06 — *King Lear*.

'07 — *Timon of Athens*.

'09 — *Coriolanus*. *Sonnets* published.

'11 — He retires from the company and comes back to his native village. *The Winter's Tale*, *The Tempest*.

'12 — *Henry VIII*.

'16 — His Last will and Testament drawn up.

— Apr. 23, Shakespeare dies on his fifty-second birth anniversary.

— Apr. 25, he is buried in the chancel of the Stratford Church.

The exact date of his birth is not known, as the register of Baptism maintained by the parish church did not record the date of birth but of baptism only. As the official language of the time was Latin, the entry in the Register says:

1564, Apr. 26, Gulielmus Filius Johannes Shakespeare.[2]

It was the custom those days to baptize a baby three days after its birth, perhaps because of the prevalence of infant mortality. It is therefore assumed that he was born on the 23rd of April, in the village of Stratford-upon-Avon, the county being Warwickshire. This was a lucky day for it was St. George's day, England's patron saint.

Not much is known about his childhood days but it can be taken for granted that he spent a happy and secure childhood in the bosom of a loving and prosperous family. His position in the family was a significant one as he was the eldest son. His father John Shakespeare was in the trade and therefore not regarded as a gentleman (i.e. belonging to the class of landed gentry), but was a worthy man in society. Later, he was to become the alderman for by this time the little village had expanded enough to have one. This was in 1565 and by this time he was in a position to claim the status of a gentleman. Keeping in mind the feudal structure of contemporary society, this fact was of great significance. Socially speaking, Shakespeare's mother came from a family belonging to a higher level, for Mary Arden's father belonged to the class of small landed gentry.

The village was surrounded by a wonderful countryside, and William, as a little boy, would run wild in the lap of benevolent Nature. The memory of this beautiful environment was to produce the lovely and lyrical passages of nature description of his poetry. The sunny glades of the forest of Arden look back to these joyful experiences, though, of course, Shakespeare mentions the freezing skies and the bitter winds of winter as well, for he was not one to shirk the reality.

Another significant fact is that his father was a Justice of Peace (vide Ch. 2, supra) as well as the high Bailiff of Stratford. He had to execute many duties connected with courts of law and Shakespeare, being the eldest son, often accompanied him. He thus gained intimate knowledge of legal procedures, of which the trial scene of the *Merchant of Venice* is the proof.

Queen Elizabeth had established grammar schools all over England in order to educate the commoners. Shakespeare was duly admitted to the local one. He was perhaps seven at this time and did not take kindly to it at all. It is therefore thought that in the passage in *As You Like It* where Jaques refers to the schoolboy, Shakespeare is referring to himself, or, at least, writing out of personal experience:

> Then the whining schoolboy, with his satchel
> And shining morning face, creeping like snail
> Unwillingly to school.[3]

Latin grammar was the most important part of the curriculum in these schools. Boys of the aristocratic class went to exclusive and expensive schools where they got classical education which Shakespeare could not get. But this does not mean that he did not get any education in the classics. Ben Jonson's ridicule of his "small Latin and less Greek" is well-known but most misleading. Shakespeare may not have been a classical scholar of good standard according to contemporary expectations, but he had acquired a fair knowledge of classical literature. Shakespeare was a student here till he was about 14 or 16, it is not known exactly when he left the school.

All these schools in England followed the same curriculum and kept the same hours. School started at six in the morning and went on till five in the evening. There were breaks during the day and there were clear-cut rules which laid down that, in all, there had to be two and a half hours' break spaced out during the day. The curriculum is given below:

Poetry: *The Bucolica* of Mantuan
The Eclogues and *The Aeneid* of Virgil.
The Poems of Horace.
The Metamorphoses of Ovid.

Prose: Caesar, Livy, Cicero.

Drama: Ten tragedies of Seneca.

The comedies of Plautus.
The comedies of Terence.

This makes it quite clear that Shakespeare had a solid foundation of classical education. The classical references that occur continuously in his plays come from first hand knowledge of classical literature. One of his biographers remarks:

> Today, all scholars agree that Shakespeare was a well-educated man of his times, that he certainly continued to further his education by wide reading throughout his life and that there is no display of learning in any one of his plays which could not have been acquired at the Stratford Grammar School.[4]

There is another opinion that goes totally against this idea of Shakespeare's schooling. It is a well-known fact that the family was a Catholic one and, basing his theory on this fact, John Dover Wilson has argued that John Shakespeare may not have put his son in the Grammar School at all. There were many great Catholic noblemen at the time and he might have sent his son to one such household. Shakespeare might have received his education and gained inside knowledge of the lifestyle of the aristocracy in this manner and depicted it in his plays.

After some years, some kind of misfortune had visited the family and John Shakespeare's fortunes went under an eclipse. Shakespeare was taken out of the school in his teens, but it is not known exactly when. It is not known whether he had completed his education by that time either. Every year, every hour of education is of crucial importance at this age, for the mind is more capable of learning at this time than at any other. How much harm it had done to Shakespeare's future career is only to be guessed at.

It was during these highly formative years that Shakespeare first came into contact with stage-performances. Many records exist of different travelling companies of players visiting his village. These itinerant groups were patronized by the great aristocrats of the time and were accordingly named after them. There were groups belonging to the Earls of Leicester, Warwick and Worcester. They staged the traditional moralities as well as the modern five-act plays written in imitation of classical models, like *Gorboduc*, etc.

While still in his teens, Shakespeare's sensitive and young mind fell to the charms of the local belle Anne Hathaway from a village that lay at a little distance, named Shottery. She was a much admired and sought after girl, as becomes clear from an anonymous couplet often quoted by his biographers:

> Anne Hathaway, she hath a way
> To charm all hearts, Anne Hathaway.

Young Shakespeare was the one on whom she bestowed her favours and agreed to marry. She was eight years older than him but this was no barrier to the lovers and they got married on Nov. 28, 1582. He was not yet nineteen, whereas she was twenty-six. Next year Susanna their first child, was born. She was baptized on May 26, 1583. Nearly two years later, the twins, Hamnet and Judith, were born. Hamnet died in 1596, leaving no one to carry on the line.

Thus, when barely twenty-one, Shakespeare was a man with three children, a wife eight years older than himself and no visible means of earning a livelihood. Nor was his father's financial position at all an enviable one. There are many versions of how he earned a livelihood at this time. John Aubrey, one of the first biographers in English, had recorded that he was teaching in a school near his own village. How far this is true is debatable. Another better-known story is given by a clergyman and the actor Thomas Betterton. This story became so widely known that it is commonly accepted as true, though it is highly debatable how much of truth there is in it. At Charlecote there was a deer park which was the property of one Sir Thomas Lucy. It is said that Shakespeare, along with some other young men, stole a deer from this park. They were all caught and it is said that Sir Thomas had ordered the young men to be whipped and put into prison. It is also said that Shakespeare resented this bitterly and took his revenge on Sir Thomas by portraying him as Justice Shallow the stupid judge in *The Merry Wives of Windsor*, and *Henry IV*. Modern researches however, have proved that this story is of doubtful authenticity, for Sir Thomas was not the master of Charlecote forest at that time. It has, however, been supposed for a long time that it was this humiliation that acted as a deciding factor behind Shakespeare's leaving Stratford in 1586, for London.

Another legend connected with this time of Shakespeare's life, is that he had joined one of the itinerant dramatic companies as an actor, spending quite a few years with it. Again, no one is sure of how much of truth there is in this story. What has given rise to it is a will left by a rich Lancashire gentleman, leaving a considerable sum to one William Shakeshafte, a player in his service. This name is suggestive, for Shakeshafte is a variant of the surname Shakespeare. Such variants were common in Elizabethan times, for English was as yet a fluid, young language, with its grammar and pronunciation not yet rigidly formulated.

It is known for sure that the dramatic group, the Queen's Men, visited Stratford at this time, and perhaps, this made Shakespeare's thoughts turn towards London. Many other groups also came there and Shakespeare had become familiar with theatrical productions while still young. In 1583, for example, three well-known groups produced plays at Stratford. Two famous and well-organized groups had come there in 1587. Many of his biographers think that he had acted in these. Hamlet's well-known conversation with the players gives evidence of first hand knowledge not only of acting but of stagecraft as well.

The period stretching from 1586 to 1592 is known as the Dark Years, for little is known of them. As actual record of facts is non-existent, anecdotes exist in great profusion. It is said that he would be loitering outside the playhouses in order to earn a little money by looking after the horses of the gentlemen who came riding to watch the plays. Another legend has said that he was a prompter's assistant. What is known for sure is that he had found a fellow villager named Richard Field who had left Stratford before Shakespeare did and had become an established printer by this time. This friend published his *Venus and Adonis* in 1593 and *The Rape of Lucrece* the next year, both of which became instantly popular. His literary career thus, had begun with narrative poems which were very popular at this time.

In the field of drama, his only serious rival at this time was Marlowe, and it is a remarkable coincidence that both of them, independently, had reached London at the same time. The two Chronological Tables given earlier show that they had been born the same year also. This decade (the eighties) was a highly prosperous and stimulating one. Sir Francis Drake was scouring the Spanish Main and Sir Philip Sidney was in the process of writing the first sequence of love-sonnets, *Astrophel and Stella.* Perhaps his monumental prose romance *Arcadia*, also, was being drafted at the same time. Out in Ireland, Spenser was composing his poetical masterpiece, *The Faerie Queene.* One by one, the members of the group of learned young men, the University Wits, were converging towards London. Lyly, the leader of the group, had already produced his *Euphues* and was now turning towards drama. Two of his romantic comedies, *Campaspe* and *Sappho and Phaon* were performed for the Queen by the choir of the Chapel Royal in 1584. It was *Euphues*, that brought him fame. It was so popular with the ladies that Lyly had declared the hope that:

> Euphues had rather lie shut in a lady's casket than open on a scholar's study.[5]

London, in other words, was the centre of cultural and other activities. Marlowe's *Tamburlaine* was presented in 1587, and by then, Shakespeare was definitely present there. It was a truly wonderful time of expansion and therefore of enthusiasm, with horizons receding farther and farther in every yield. This was the London to which Shakespeare came. F.E. Halliday remarks:

> Shakespeare had arrived in London at the most thrilling moment in its history; thrilling, however, not only because of danger, anxiety, expectation and hope in the air, but also because the long-awaited dramatic revival was now imminent.[6]

Shakespeare watched and avidly learned from, the plays that were being staged, perhaps acting minor parts in them. He must have been consolidating his position in literacy London slowly but surely because his works had become important enough to be noticed by such a well established University Wit as Greene. It is he who is always cited as being the first contemporary to have mentioned Shakespeare's name. It occurs in a pamphlet remembered today chiefly for this reason, named *Greene's Groats-worth of Wit Bought with a Million of Repentance*. At the end of this, there is a letter addressed to Peele, Nashe and, of course, Marlowe. He warns them against actors, particularly against a certain actor, in a highly allusive manner. There can be no doubt that the reference is to Shakespeare whom he ridicules and castigates in offensive terms:

> Yes, trust them not: for there is an upstart crow, beautified with our feathers that with his Tyger's heart wrapt in a Player's hyde, supposes he is as well able to bombast out a blank verse as the best of you: and being an absolute Johannes Factotum, is in his own conceit the only shake-scene in a country.[7]

Two clear clues hint at our poet in this famous sentence. The line "Tyger's heart wrapt in a player's hyde" is a deliberate misquotation of Shakespeare's line "O tiger's heart wrapped in a woman's hide" in *Henry VI*, Pt. III. Next, there is the word "shake-scene" which is a sarcastic reference to our poet's name. This kind of reference speaks volumes about Greene's spitefulness and jealousy, but also makes it clear that by this time, Shakespeare had become important enough to cause alarm to the reigning dramatists. This reference occurred in 1592 and from now onwards, there are frequent bits of information on him. To have made a mark in six years is no mean achievement for the ignorant country yokel as he must have appeared to the sophisticated and well-established University Wits.

At this time, he was still learning his craft and these years are known as the years of apprenticeship. He was, however, not merely learning, but producing also. The sonnet-sequence to Mr. W.H., the two narrative poems, the *Henry VI* trilogy, *Richard III*, *Titus Andronicus*, *The Comedy of Errors*. *The Two Gentlemen of Verona* and *The Taming of the Shrew* were all churned out at this time. They were all highly successful. It seems surprising today that an unsubtle blood-and-thunder tragedy like *Titus Andronicus* was so popular in its day that it was published in 1594 and the title-page reveals its success:

> ...as it was played by the Rt Hon. the Earl of Derby, the Earl of Pembroke and the Earl of Sussex their servants.[8]

These three were all well-known companies. It is also clear that they had put it up in quick succession.

The list given above is significant also as it shows that Shakespeare had not confined his talent to any particular genre. Kyd and Marlowe had written only tragedies. Shakespeare, from the very beginning, was able to produce successful comedies (*The Two Gentlemen of Verona*) tragedies (*Titus Andronicus*) and histories in the field of drama itself let alone that of sonnets and poems. Marlowe had already been killed by 1594 and Shakespeare had proved his versatility as well as stage-worthiness.

By this time, he had joined the group of Lord Chamberlaine's Men, and had become an important member of it. This can be surmised because at this time, the company had produced two plays at Court and the receipt of payment issued by the Royal Treasury contains the names of Shakespeare, Kempe and Burbage. Shakespeare remained in this company till the very end of his life. It was a case of a very happy symbiosis, for a company needed a good writer of its own in order to be in a state of continuous productivity, and a writer, of course, needed a company to produce his plays.

It is thought that he had paid a visit to Stratford at this time. Shakespeare's father, in his sixties, was the head of a big family, surrounded by his children and grandchildren. Shakespeare himself was twenty-eight and his children were growing up. Susanna was nine and the twins were seven. It was time for Hamnet to start school. Shakespeare stayed in the bosom of his family for four months and it is thought that he wrote *Richard III* and *Venus and Adonis* during this visit. The poem was dedicated to the Earl of Southampton, the supposed "onlie begetter" of the sonnet-sequence.

Shakespeare was lucky to find a patron like the young Earl of Southampton to himself. He was a well-known patron of arts and, soon enough, a deep and intense friendship developed between them. The sonnets speak eloquently of this relationship, though there is no way of proving it in any other way. The Earl, not named anywhere in the sequence, is designated as Mr. W.H. in the "Dedication" and it is thought that these are the initials of Henry Wriothesely (The Earl of Southampton) in reversed order. The sonnets also describe a nameless Dark Lady with whom Shakespeare was in love. There follows a harrowing account of how Mr. W.H. and the Dark Lady together betrayed Shakespeare. How much of this is true cannot be known for sure but Shakespeare's intense love for Mr. W.H. is quite apparent. It has been expressed in the passionate tradition of Courtly Love.

Though the story told by the sonnets may not have much biographical relevance, it is quite true that Shakespeare enjoyed the patronage of the Earl of Southampton. He had dedicated the two narrative poems in addition to the sonnets to his patron. "The Dedication" in *The Rape of Lucrece* is instinct with the worshipful adoration he had towards Mr. W.H.:

> The love I dedicate to your Lordship is without end... what I have done is yours, what I have to do is yours, being part in all I have devoted yours.[9]

The patronage of the Earl gave his life the security that is so necessary for an artist. He was able to buy a share in his own company—the money, it is believed, being supplied by the Earl. In those times, a poet had to have patronage in order to survive, unless, of course, he had some other source of income. Shakespeare was fortunate indeed. At this time, Greene was languishing in poverty and sickness, whereas Shakespeare was buying property. A.L. Rowse remarks:

> It meant all the difference between the dreadful insecurity poor Greene had, and others, died of and having firm ground under his feet.[10]

His company, having him for its writer, soon became the leading company in London. Apart from public performances, it gave thirty-two stagings in Queen Elizabeth's Court, a rare distinction for any theatrical company.

How prosperous and successful Shakespeare was can be understood only if we take a look at the literary perspective of the time. First of all, he was the only dramatist to survive the terrible havoc wrought by the Plague. Kyd was already dead at thirty-five years of age and Marlowe who was his most serious rival, was killed suddenly at a drunken brawl. Greene was dead at thirty-four years, and Peele would die in a few years. Lyly and Lodge had almost come to the end of their productivity. Nashe had turned to pamphlets in preference to plays. Ben Jonson, the only dramatist of a calibre like his own, had still not come. Shakespeare's star was in the ascendant at the moment.

The highly entertaining early comedies now poured forth. A successful man-about-town, he was enjoying life to the full and it is thought that Lord Berowne, the gayest and wittiest Lord in *Love's Labour's Lost* is, as Halliday describes, "a half-mocking and unconscious projection of himself." This was the year of 1594, and he was thirty years old, in the full vigour of energetic creativity. A literary mention of his name occurs in a poem by an Oxford undergraduate, one Henry Willoughby. He mentions Shakespeare as one who gives good advice about love-affairs. The poet particularly mentions his narrative poem:

> Yet Tarquin plucked his glistering grape
>
> And Shakespeare paints poor Lucrece's rape.[11]

In 1597, Shakespeare had the tragic experience of losing his only son and heir Hamnet. He was writing *King John* at the time. His father had, earlier, applied at the Herald's College for a coat-of-arms without any success and Shakespeare now pursued the matter. This would give his family the status of a gentleman—a matter of great importance in the feudal society of the time. This time the request was granted and when our poet came back to London as a gentleman, he also bought New Place which was the second best house in Stratford, the first being the Town Hall. Stratford was no longer a little village, it had expanded into a big enough place to require a Town Hall. This gives an idea of Shakespeare's status.

By 1598, he was acknowledged as a master dramatist. A well-known document of the time named *Palladis Tamia* written by Francis Meres gives an eulogistic account of his works:

> ...the sweet wittie soule of Ovid lives in mellifluous and hony-tonged Shakespeare , witness his Venus and Adonis his Lucrece, his sugred sonnets among his friends.[12]

This work gives a list of the plays that had been written and staged to date. This list is of great help to scholars in determining the dates of his works. Meres's attitude is a pointer to the high esteem in which Shakespeare was held. He asserts that Shakespeare is the contemporary equivalent of Terence and Plautus in comedy and of Seneca in tragedy.

Not only was Shakespeare acclaimed as the best dramatist of the time, but his company also got recognition. The Queen passed away in 1603 and King James VI of Scotland acceeded to the throne of England as King James I. He took the Lord Chamberlaine's men under his own patronage and the company was named as the King's Men. This was a coveted position—in fact the highest honour for any group. The members of the company would have the royal livery to wear and take part in all royal pageants and processions.

There are many records of Shakespeare's life from this point onwards. He had become well-settled in London. Legal documents prove that he went on changing his dwelling-place, staying at Bishopgate in 1595, at Southwark in 1599, at Cripple-gate in 1604. He bought a house at Blackfriars in 1613 though he did not occupy it. In 1602, he acquired a hundred and seven acres of land for farming and later in the same year, he bought a cottage and a quarter acre of land. He continued to write for his company and also acted in it, for there existed a record that showed he had acted in Ben Jonson's *Sejanus*, a historical tragedy performed by his company in 1603.

He returned to Stratford in 1603 when there was another plague in London. His great tragedies were now produced. *Hamlet* was staged in 1602 the last play he wrote in the Elizabethan age. In 1604, *Othello*, the first of his Jacobean plays, was performed at court. The chronicles and the problem plays were all written in the Jacobean age. There is a great difference in spirit between the Elizabethan and the Jacobean age. As Theodore Spencer has pointed out, the Renaissance optimism was succeeded by the Jacobean age of conflict and pessimism. A sombre evaluation of life and person succeeded exuberance and enthusiasm. As Theodore Spencer has remarked:

> The earlier Renaissance had emphasized man's potentialities by comparing man with the angels; the later Renaissance emphasized their destruction by comparing man with the animals.[13]

The plays Shakespeare wrote at this time reflect this sombre attitude. The tragedies and the problem plays reflect the very spirit of the age in that they reflect upon the spirit of man and the nature of evil.

By now, Shakespeare was spending his summers regularly at Stratford. In 1608, his mother passed away and his first grandchild was born. Both of these are events of moment, signifying the onset of age. In three more years (1611), he would leave London and settle at Stratford.

As the years passed, he left the turbulent waters of the problem comedies and the tragedies behind him and emerged into the deep serenity of the last romances. The sonnet-sequence was published in 1609 and in 1611 (according to Irving Ribner and others), he retired to Stratford.

His connections with London, however, were not severed. He continued coming there on matters of business. For example, he got the Blackfriar Gate House in 1613, and his name continued to appear in various documents. He kept up his connections with the stage for at the end of 1612 *The Tempest* was performed to celebrate a royal betrothal. It is said that he himself enacted the role of Prospero and blessed the couple.

His health was failing, though it is not well-known what he was suffering from. In 1616, his will was drawn up and can still be seen in Somerset House. This was in February and two months later, on 23rd April which was his birthday, he passed away at fifty-four years of age.

Many rich and complex symbols adorn his grave. There is a bust of himself with a quill in his hand, signifying that he was a writer. Corinthian columns stand at the sides with a cornice on them. The allegorical figures of Rest and Labour adorn this cornice. His coat-of-arms is placed between these two figures and the whole thing is surmounted by a skull. There is a memorial tablet with a Latin couplet and a sextet in English. The grave itself bears an epitaph in the form of a quatrain. It is thought that this was written by the poet himself, though many scholars think that it is a bit too crude to have been his own work. This is how it runs:

> Good friend, for Jesus sake forbeare
> To dig the dust enclosed here!
> Blest be the man that spares these stones
> And curst be he that moves my bones.[14]

(b) Shakespeare's Works

A tentative scheme of Shakespeare's works has been drawn up by his critics and biographers. This has been based on contemporary documents like Henslowe's Diary, the Stationer's Register and others. These recorded the dates of the performances on stage, not of composition or of publications. Again, the dates of performances of many plays are not known and, to make the whole thing even more confusing, some of the plays like *Titus Andronicus* were published quite early, and some much later. Notwithstanding these difficulties, a scheme has been more or less agreed upon, though the stages cannot really be strictly demarcated.

Phase I

1591 — *The Comedy of Errors.*

'92 — *The Two Gentlemen of Verone*, *Henry VI*, Parts I, II and III.

'93 — *King Richard III*, *Romeo and Juliet*, *Venus and Adonis*.

Phase II

'94 — *The Rape of Lucrece*, *The Sonnets*, *Titus Andronicus*, *King Richard II*, *A Midsummer Night's Dream*, *Love's Labour's Lost*, *King John*, *The Taming of the Shrew*.

'95 — *The Merchant of Venice*.

'97 — *Henry IV*, Pt I.

'98 — *Henry IV*, Pt II, *The Merry Wives of Windsor*.

'99 — *Henry V*, *Much Ado About Nothing*, *Julius Caesar*.

1600 — *As You Like It*, *Twelfth Night*.

Phase III

'02 — *Hamlet*, *Troilus and Cressida*, *All's Well That Ends Well*.

'04 — *Measure for Measure*, *Othello*.

'05 — *King Lear*.

'06 — *Macbeth*.

'07 — *Antony and Cleopatra*.

'08 — *Coriolanus*, *Timon of Athens*, *Pericles*.

Phase IV

'10 — *Cymbeline*, *The Winter's Tale*, *The Tempest*.

'11 — *Henry VIII*.

As this table shows, Shakespeare's career has been divided into four phases, though these are not mutually exclusive. Some critics, for example, think that all the works up to *Love's Labour's Lost* belong to the first phase, while some say that *Pericles* belongs to the fourth phase, not the third. These are matters of opinion. The first phase is known as the Phase of Experiment or of Apprenticeship, from 1591 to 1594 or perhaps to 1595. At this time he was busy re-writing or revising plays that were already in existence—the best way for learning one's craft. He made frequent use of couplets and end-stopped lines at this time, as can be seen, for example, in *A Midsummer*

Night's Dream. Exuberant word-play can be seen in *Love's Labour's Lost*. The art of characterization has not developed yet, though he balances his characters against each other quite expertly.

The period of development stretches from 1594-95 to 1601. He produced the Golden Comedies (of which *As You Like It* is thought to be the best) and the Chronicles during this time. He has attained mastery over blank verse and has started to plumb the depths of the human mind in his portrayal of characters. The plots too, are handled with expertise.

The third phase ended in 1608. One can see a definite change of attitude in the work of this period. The witty and light-hearted characters are no longer there. Instead, he had started looking evil in the face, evil in humanity as well as in Nature:

> The conflict between good and evil, ugliness and beauty, innocence and crime, purity and impurity, hope and disgust, love and hate, order and disorder, natural laws and the anarchy produced by the passions—all is resolved in Shakespeare's so-called "dark period" with an infinite despair.[15]

The problem comedies and the Great tragedies belong to this period.

From 1608 till 1612 is the last phase or the Romance period during which the last four Romances were written. Shakespeare has now achieved the wisdom that comes with age, a calm acceptance of the presence of evil as inevitable and a looking forward to the future with hope that a new generation will create a better world. Fluchere remarks:

> As his career draws to a close Shakespeare turned back to his youth, and his implicit theme is always that of fertility, resurrection, joy of life.[16]

The four Romances were followed by two more plays. Even up to the twentieth century, there had been controversy about the chronicle play *King Henry VIII*. Nowadays, however, scholars agree in ascribing it to him. *The Two Noble Kinsmen*, it has always been known, was a work of collaboration with Fletcher.

The time has now come to cast a passing glance at his works. In the brief notes on his plays and poems that shall now be given, it has been tried to follow a roughly chronological order. As the dates of composition, performance and publication differ, it is difficult, not to say impossible, to be exact.

(c) Brief Notes on His Works

The Comedy of Errors

This play is his shortest, and was staged in 1594. There are many critics who think this to be the first of his works. The plot is from Plautus's rollicking comedy *The Menaechmuses* in which there is but one pair of twins and Shakespeare has doubled this. Consequently the intrigues as well as the cases of mistaken identities have multiplied. The only theme that gains prominence is that of the relationship between husband and wife, which Shakespeare will deal with in detail later on, in *The Taming of the Shrew*.

The Two Gentlemen of Verona

This play is usually looked upon as the first of his romantic comedies. There are two pairs of lovers, two servants and two fathers. The characters, thus, are balanced against each other and make a symmetrical pattern. Conflict between love and friendship is the theme and the emphasis falls on friendship. There is also the theme of forgiveness and reconciliation that will occupy the poet so intensely in the last romances. Many features of his mature comedies, like crossed love, disguised heroines, exile, flight, etc. appear in this play, Julia is a precursor of Rosalind and Portia, and Silvia of Juliet.

Henry VI, Parts, I, II and III

This trilogy begins the chronicles that brought Shakespeare so much renown. He wrote ten such plays, including *Henry VIII*. These are not mere records of historical events but the serious issues of the duties and privileges of kings are also dealt with. He presented their human as well as ceremonial aspects, with all the pomp and pageantry it involved.

These plays were staged in 1592 and became so popular that the entire trilogy was performed three times in eight days.

Greene had referred to one of the lines (vide p. 22, *supra*). It presents a world of ferocity and ends in regicide.

Richard III

The early poetry of Shakespeare shows the influence of Marlowe. *The Henry VI* trilogy showed this quite clearly and in this play the influence can be seen not only in poetry but in characterization as well. Richard III the hero is a Marlovian figure and the play too is more like a tragedy than a history play. It is the second longest play of Shakespeare and extremely effective on the stage. Many critics group this play with the *Henry VI* trilogy and call the entire sequence a tetralogy. Yet the figure of the King dominates the play and his woeful fate makes the play a tragedy, evoking pity and terror.

Romeo and Juliet

This is one of his most popular tragedies, telling the story of star-crossed lovers. The hero and the heroine have become the archetypes of unfortunate lovers. This, like the Greek tragedies is a tragedy of fate, with family feud taking the place of fate. Shakespeare has not yet perfected his art of characterization to the extent when it can be said that in his tragedies, character is destiny. Instead, he has followed the original story very closely. Some of the speeches and scense in it have become classics, particularly the Queen Mab speech by Mercutio and the Balcony scene between the lovers.

Venus and Adonis

Narrative poems based on classical myths were very popular at that time and Shakespeare's became an instant hit. He took the story from Ovid, and the poem ran through ten or eleven editions in his own lifetime. He had many good models before him, particularly those by the university wits. Narrative poetry was a new genre for him, but he shows himself a master at it. He has written it in sextains, i.e. a quatrain followed by a couplet. This is well-suited for narrative poetry and easier to handle than the nine-line form used by Spenser in his *Faerie Queene*, which Shakespeare must have read.

The Rape of Lucrece

This is the second of his long narrative poems and resembles *Venus and Adonis* in two other matters also—it is dedicated to the Earl of Southampton and is based on Ovid. This is a much more serious poem than the former one, for Shakespeare tries to analyse the feeling of guilt in Tarquin. This psychological insight raises the poem above the light-hearted narratives that were fashionable at the time. Tarquin's conflicts of emotion raise him to tragic heights. Shakespeare has given proof of his poetic craft by using the rhyme royal form.

The Sonnets

This is a sequence of a hundred and fifty-four love-sonnets instinct with intense passion. They, as had been mentioned above (*vide* his Life, *supra*) are supposed to be autobiographical, depicting the relationship between himself and the Earl of Southampton whom he designates as Mr. W.H., "the onlie begetter" of these sonnets. The first 126 of the sonnets are addressed to him and the remaining to the equally famous Dark Lady, who was perhaps Mary Fitton, a maid of honour at Court. Usually Elizabethan love-sonnets were addressed to one person, and Shakespeare's sequence is unique in that it explores a triangular situation.

Titus Andronicus

This play is a Roman tragedy and also a revenge tragedy. It follows Seneca and Kyd and can be rightfully called a blood-and-thunder tragedy. It contains a well-known parody of a famous passage in Kyd's *The Spanish Tragedy*, and was extremely popular at that time.

Richard II

This play, unlike others, has a certain topical relevance. It reflects the political situation of the time so graphically that the Queen had been extremely annoyed and said, "I am Richard II, know ye that? This tragedy is played forty times in open streets and houses." The play shows the deposition of King Richard II and this was such a sensitive issue that the scene had to be omitted when the play was staged.

A Midsummer Night's Dream

This is undoubtedly the best among his early comedies. It has been a very popular from the beginning and continues to be so. In it, for the first time, Shakespeare introduces the supernatural element in the characters of the fairy King and Queen and their attendants. The range of characters in the play, therefore, is wider than it had formerly been, and will be equalled only by *The Tempest* at the end of his career. The story goes back to the pagan times of Greece.

Love's Labour's Lost

This play has always been notable for its witty dialogues. All the characters are witty, but Lord Berowne is the wittiest of all. The characters are all from high aristocracy, there being the French King, the Princess to whom he pays court, four courtiers and four ladies. In the subplot humbler characters have been introduced. As has been pointed out in the Life given above, the character of the happy-go-lucky, light-hearted and witty Lord Berowne is supposed to be half-autobiographical. A passage by him, renouncing flowery and ornate diction, has become famous.

King John

This play is centred round the historical figure of King John, but, indirectly, it has a topical relevance as well. King John had waged a life-long battle with the Church of Rome and Queen Elizabeth had done the same. This had ultimately resulted in her excommunication by the Pope. Shakespeare has always avoided religious issues and this is the only play in which he has taken it up. In spite of this, the play is not a religious one. It is actually a highly patriotic play in which foreign policy is treated as the most important theme. The character of King John has been depicted with great insight. Shakespeare shows himself well able to deal with such issues.

The Taming of the Shrew

This play was performed in 1594 and has an Italian setting. The main characters, the hero and the heroine, have been strongly and effectively sketched in. The central theme is the relationship between husband and wife, both of them aiming at supremacy over the other, an extremely popular theme of his day. It is a most entertaining and stage-worthy play. Shakespeare, always mindful of neatly balancing his characters, has created another female character as foil for the shrew. This throws both the characters into relief. Shakespeare's talent for creating convincing characters is amply in evidence.

The Merchant of Venice

This is the first of his Golden comedies. The merchant of the title should, according to custom, be the hero, but it is doubtful whether he can really be called so. As a matter of fact, Shylock, the villain of the piece, is such a forceful character that he towers over everyone else. One of the most important female characters Portia, is the heroine of this play. Shakespeare makes extensive and effective use of the Elizabethan convention of disguise, for each of the three female characters don male disguises, though for a very short time. He also shows full mastery over blank verse and poetic diction in this play, using different kinds of diction for different scenes and characters.

Henry IV, Parts I and II

These two plays are the crowning achievements of English Chronicle plays. Sir John Falstaff has become the archetype of comic characters. Towards the end of the play Prince Hal accedes to the throne as King Henry V and leaving his days of jollity behind him, devotes himself to the duties of kingship in earnest. He has to dissociate himself from the past and therefore rejects Falstaff who had been his boon companion all these days. Though his rejection of Falstaff is fully understandable and even commendable, the cruel manner of doing it creates a lasting impression in the audience. Falstaff, however, has become immortal.

The Merry Wives of Windsor

Queen Elizabeth was so charmed by Falstaff that she ordered a play with "the fat knight in love" and Shakespeare produced this. This rollicking farce begins at the point where Henry IV, Pt. 2 ends, i.e. with Falstaff's rejection. It is a highly entertaining and stage-worthy play but has not attracted serious critical attention. One feature of the play is significant. It seems that Shakespeare had poked fun at Ben Jonson's humour characters. Corporal Nym is a parody of such a character, for he uses the word "humour" in almost every sentence he speaks.

King Henry V

Shakespearean scholars say that this play presents Shakespeare's concept of the ideal king. Kingship and patriotism are the twin themes of the play. Shakespeare deals with the historical battle of Agincourt in which the English won a resounding victory over the French. Shakespeare does not glorify war in a partisan manner, but, with the insight of a true poet, presents the positive as well as the negative side of war—bravery and endurance as well as death and suffering. Henry V shows himself as a strict but just King. Falstaff goes to Arthur's bosom in this play.

Much Ado About Nothing

This play is the second in the group of his four Golden Comedies. Like almost all Elizabethan comedies, it has more than one plot and the theme is love. Shakespeare has presented the theme in two different ways. There is crude physical love which is based on appearances that prove to be deceptive. This aspect of love is presented in the Hero-Claudio plot. The Benedick-Beatrice plot takes up the theme of the rejection of married love that Shakespeare takes up repeatedly in his plays. As in the other comedies, the lovers gradually come to accept the social responsibilities of marriage though, at first, they are not conscious of this.

Julius Caesar

This play has been designated, along with *Coriolanus* and *Antony and Cleopatra*, as a Roman tragedy. The central theme of the play is the opposition of tyranny and liberty. It is a stern play with a stern plot which has but little of comedy in it. His characters, though historical, are all living and convincing human beings. He took the story from Lord North's translation of Plutarch's famous *Lives*. Shakespeare adapted many of the prose passages in this book into blank verse. This shows his resourcefulness. Supernatural elements are presented in the figure of Caesar's Ghost.

As You Like It

This play is avowedly the best of the Golden Comedies. More than half of the play is located in the pastoral environment of the forest of Arden and this has led to its being labelled as a pastoral comedy. Love, the central theme as in all romantic comedies, is presented in four different ways through four pairs of lovers. There are royal and courtly characters as well as humble shepherds. At the end of the play, all are neatly paired off, with four marriages in the last scene. Rosalind is one of the most charming heroines and her use of a male disguise produces some effective examples of dramatic irony. It also affords an example of the manner in which Shakespeare adopts a popular convention when it suits him.

Twelfth Night

This play succeeds *As You Like It. Twelfth Night* is the fourth and the last of the Golden Comedies. All the conventional elements of popular comedies are present in it: disguises, mistaken identities, the separation and re-union of siblings, etc. Shakespeare makes the plot even more complicated by making the separated siblings identical twins. A watered-down version of Falstaff is to be found in Sir Toby Belch, and one of the most remarkable jesters, Feste, is presented in this play. He is a highly accomplished jester, surpassed only by the unique Fool in *king Lear*. Viola is one of the most charming heroines of our poet.

Troilus and Cressida

This is the first of the Problem Comedies, and Shakespeare turns to Ancient Greece for his source material. These are all plays that deal with the most unattractive traits of human beings, presenting the seamy side of life. This particular play comes very near to a satire and gives a satirical, disillusioned treatment to the two themes of love and war.

All's Well That Ends Well

The second of the Problem Comedies, this play deals with the theme of the conflict between virtue and nobility. This is seen in the Bertram-Helena plot but there are several sub-themes, like the conflict between old and young generations. In this play, Shakespeare is far less tolerant of the follies and vices of humanity than he had been earlier. There is a marked difference between the braggart soldier Parolles and Falstaff.

Measure for Measure

Another Problem Comedy, this is a very serious play though like *As You Like It*, the merriest of the Golden Comedies, it ends with four marriages. The themes of justice and fidelity are the twin themes of the play. It contains one of the most charming songs of Shakespeare.

Othello

Hamlet was the last Elizabethan tragedy that Shakespeare had written, and *Othello* is the first of his Jacobean plays and the second of the four Great Tragedies. It has been called the *Romeo and Juliet* of his later phase and treats the theme of jealousy. One of his most important villains, Iago, comes in this play about whom the famous phrase "motiveless malignity" has been used by Coleridge.

King Lear

This is the play regarded at present as the greatest of his tragedies. It depicts, not merely the follies of King Lear and his tragic fate, but the predicaments of man himself in a cruel universe. The play has therefore been called a cosmic drama. A primitive legend has been transformed into a terrible tragedy that has the qualities of sublimity and universality in it. One of the unique characters in it is that of the Fool who serves many complex purposes. Dante's *Divine Comedy* is one of the works with which this play has been compared.

Macbeth

Shakespeare chose a story from Scottish history for this tragedy, thus paying a tribute to the Scottish King James I. It is well-known as the darkest and gloomiest of his tragedies. One of the most important characters in it is that of Lady Macbeth. He has also used supernatural elements in it.

Antony and Cleopatra

This is a sequel to *Julius Caesar*, though it is totally different in theme. It is the theme of love that he has taken up here. The character of Cleopatra dominates the play. It is so complex that it has variously been called a history, a symphony, a political play and a Roman tragedy.

Coriolanus

This is a political Roman tragedy, the last of his tragedies. Critics usually group it with the two other Roman tragedies, *Julius Caesar* and *Antony and Cleopatra*. The hero is so intrinsically noble that he is in conflict with society and therefore, society rejects him. This brings about his tragic doom.

Timon of Athens

Though this is a five-act Problem Comedy, it is generally felt that this is not a complete play. It ends with the hero's (who is a misanthrope) withdrawal from society, but this is no fitting end and leaves a feeling of incompleteness in the mind.

Pericles, Cymbeline, The Winter's Tale, The Tempest

This group is known as the last Romances and the same theme, repeatedly, occurs in them. This is the theme of sin, repentance and forgiveness. Alongside this runs the theme of a tainted and chastened older generation handing the future over to a newer, purer younger generation. *The Tempest* is his last play, acted to celebrate a royal betrothal. Shakespeare had acted in the role of Prospero and blessed the royal couple. Prospero's renunciation is thought to be Shakespeare's farewell to the theatre.

Henry VIII

Modern scholars agree in attributing this play to Shakespeare though this had been a matter of controversy for a long time. It takes up the theme of patience in adversity. Not only does the King himself learn patience but so do the other characters as well. It ends with an affirmation of the continuity of life.

The Two Noble Kinsmen

This is a work of collaboration with Fletcher. Shakespeare wrote the major parts of Act I and also parts of Acts III and V. Many of his contemporaries had collaborated with others, but this is the only such work of Shakespeare. When Fletcher introduced a rather vulgar sub-plot Shakespeare left off working with him. The story is taken from Chaucer.

NOTES

1. The dates for these works have been taken from *The New Caxton Encyclopaedia*, London: Caxton Pubs. Ltd., 1982, 20 Vols.
2. Cited in F.E. Halliday, *The Life of Shakespeare*. London: Gerald Duckworth & Co. Ltd., 1961, p. 20.
3. *As You Like It*, Act II, scene vii, ll. 145-47, p. 38. Wae, Wordsworth Classics, 1993.
4. Irving Ribner, *William Shakespeare: Life, Timed and Theatre*, London: John Wiley and Sons Inc., 1969, pp. 38-39.
5. H. Craig, *op. cit*, p. 52, Citation.
6. F.E. Halliday, *op. cit.*, p. 60.
7. Quoted in I. Ribner, *op. cit.*, p. 45.
8. Quoted in A.L. Rowse, *William Shakespeare; A Biography*, London: Macmillan & Co. Ltd., 1963, p. 100.
9. Quoted in Halliday, *op. cit.*, pp. 102-03.
10. A.L. Rowse, *op. cit.*, p. 201.
11. Halliday, *op. cit.*, p. 118.
12. *Ibid.*, p. 138, Ribner, *op. cit.*, p. 52 and many others.
13. Theodore Spencer, *Shakespeare and the Nature of Man*. New York: The Macmillan Company, 1945, p. 49.
14. Quoted in Ribner, *op. cit.*, p. 64, and by many others.
15. H. Fluchere, *Shakespeare*, London: Longman & Green, 1953, p. 54.
16. *Ibid.*, p. 265.

3

A Brief Outline and the Genre

(a) A Brief Outline of the Story

It is a well-known fact that tragedies are hero-centred plays and this is, perhaps, more true of *Hamlet* than of any other tragedy of Shakespeare. The entire play is built around him to such an extent that any discussion of the play ultimately turns out to be a discussion of his character.

Hamlet, then, tells the story of Hamlet, the Prince of Denmark, who should actually have been the King of Denmark, for his father the former king is dead. His mother, Queen Gertrude, is still the queen, for she has married King Claudius, who is her husband's brother. This is a source of great resentment to Hamlet, though it does not seem to have caused any disturbance in the Court or anywhere else. No one talks about the marriage; everyone but Hamlet has taken it for granted. Hamlet, however, resents it so intensely that he insists on wearing deep mourning for his father, though the proper time for mourning is over.

The Ghost of Hamlet's father then appears and reveals a terrible secret to him—he had been killed by his brother Claudius. Hamlet's instinctive dislike of his uncle is now justified. Claudius has not only killed his father, but married his mother as well. As it is, Hamlet had been looking upon Claudius as a traitor, for he had dishonoured the dead by marrying his wife, but now he is revealed as a murderer as well. The Ghost then enjoins on him the sacred duty of avenging the unnatural death of his father. This is a terrible burden, for revenge is forbidden by Christianity. Hamlet, thus, is torn between filial duty and the dictates of religion. The Ghost, however, also tells him not to harm his mother. It is noticeable that he does not blame her.

Hamlet is distracted, driven almost out of his wits by all these revelations. His behaviour makes others think that he has become truly mad, and Hamlet encourages this belief. Indeed, it has long been a matter of dispute whether he is actually mad or just pretending to be, as he tells the Queen. He had been in love with Ophelia, the daughter of Polonius, the Lord Chancellor, and everyone thinks that her rejection of him has turned him mad. Ophelia also thinks so and feels guilty.

At first, Hamlet is rather skeptical about the Ghost's reality. It may have been a devil in disguise, and it may really have been his father's unquiet soul. He decides to be perfectly sure of his uncle's guilt before killing him. As luck would have it, he gets the chance for doing this. A troupe of players visit the palace, wanting to perform a play. Hamlet makes them perform *The Murder of Gonzago*, a play that parallels the events of the elder Hamlet's death, which is already part of the repertoire of this troupe. He makes some significant alterations in this play so that it may tally more with the actual events that took place. He thinks that when Claudius sees the play, he will not be able to control himself:

> I have heard
> That guilty creatures sitting at a play
> Have by the very cunning of the scene
> Been struck so to the soul, that presently
> They have proclaim'd their malefactions.[1]

This is exactly what happens. Claudius, on seeing his own treachery being enacted on the stage gets up and leaves the place in a hurry as soon as the player king is killed. The rest of the play was to have shown how the player queen betrays her dead husband and marries the murderer. This, however, is not shown as both Claudius and Queen Gertrude leave and everyone leaves with them. Hamlet is elated, for the Ghost is proved right.

Though his guilty conscience pains him, the king does not lose his head. He guesses that somehow Hamlet has come to know that he had murdered his own brother, the elder Hamlet. He then hatches a plan to get rid of him. He plans to send Hamlet to England, accompanied by Rosencrantz and Guildenstern. Then, troubled by his conscience, he kneels down to pray. It so happens that Hamlet, on his way to his mother's room (she had called him) sees him praying. He realizes that he can kill him now but he puts it off, saying that if he kills the king while he is praying, his soul will ascend to heaven which he Hamlet, definitely does not want.

He then goes to meet his mother. Unknown to him, Polonius has hidden himself behind the curtains in the room. Hamlet speaks quite roughly and cruelly to the Queen. She is frightened and cries out and Polonius taking fright at her cries, also shouts out from behind the curtains. Hamlet draws his sword and runs him through, killing him instantly. He has, of course, mistaken Polonius for the king.

He then proceeds to harangue his mother accusing her of having betrayed his father by marrying her brother-in-law. The Queen is overcome with remorse and at this point, the Ghost makes his last appearance. He tells Hamlet not to delay the revenge and also to look after the Queen. She, of course, cannot see him and Hamlet's dialogue with the invisible and inaudible Ghost confirms her belief that he is mad. She is all the more concerned for him.

After he leaves her, she tells Claudius how her mad son has killed Polonius. This does but give Claudius a valid excuse for sending Hamlet out of this country, off to England. He tells Hamlet that it is for his own good that he is being sent off. He has, however, decided to get rid of Hamlet once and for all and has entrusted to Rosencrantz and Guildenstern an official letter, duty sealed, from himself to the king of England, asking him to put Hamlet to death. Thus, Hamlet departs for England, with Rosencrantz and Guildenstern carrying, all unawares, his death-warrant.

Meanwhile, Ophelia has become mad. It should be remembered that Polonius had told her much earlier in the play (Act I, sc. iii) not to encourage Hamlet's advances. Indeed, her brother Laertes had also advised her to do the same. Then when everyone started to think that Hamlet had run mad though it was for his unrequited love for her. Ophelia herself also thought the same and blamed herself. Now he has killed her father and is departed to England. Her brother, too is in France and she is all alone. She has no one to turn to in her grief. Thus, blaming herself for Hamlet's madness and for her father's death, she has become mad. Claudius lays his finger on it when he says:

> O, this is the poison of deep grief; it springs
> All from her father's death.[2]

Laertes comes back from France, raises the populace and invades the palace, bent upon avenging his father's death. He, of course, takes the king to be guilty of having murdered his father. His grief and rage are intensified on seeing the pitiable condition of his sister and he swears vengeance upon the murderer of his father. Claudius takes this heaven-sent opportunity to tell him that it is actually Hamlet who is responsible for all these misfortunes that have visited his family. Even while they are talking, news comes that Hamlet is back in Denmark. Claudius and Laertes then hatch a plot for killing Hamlet. Laertes and he are to fight a duel and Laertes will poison the tip of his sword. Claudius also says that he will keep a cup of poisoned wine ready for Hamlet, so that if Laeres misses him, he will die by drinking the poisoned wine. They make Hamlet's death doubly sure.

Hamlet, meanwhile, having his suspicions, had secretly read Claudius's letter to the English king and replaced it with one of his own in which the English king had been asked to kill the two courtiers, Rosencrantz and Guildenstern. After this, a pirate ship had attacked Hamlet's ship and he himself had been taken prisoner. Now, on having been paid a ransom, they have set him free and he is back in Denmark.

Ophelia, meanwhile, has died by drowning. As she was mad, it cannot be called suicide—it is an accident. Hamlet reaches the cemetery in which a grave is being dug for her and here, on the open grave, Hamlet and Laertes meet. They at once come to blows, are separated and a formal duel is then arranged. They shall meet, it is decided, in front of the King and the Queen, and fight a duel like true sportsmen. Bets are laid and Hamlet is confirmed of winning. There is no enmity for Laertes in his mind.

The court enters and the conditions for the duel are laid down by Claudius. The cup of poisoned wine is put there and the Queen, ignorant of its true nature, drinks from it. Now her death is assured. Then, as they fight, Laertes wounds Hamlet with his poisoned rapier and Hamlet's death also becomes a certainty. As they continue duelling, the two combatants change their rapiers so that Hamlet has Laertes's poisoned one. He wounds Laertes with it. By this time, the poison has started its work on the Queen and Claudius tries to pass it off. But she has understood that the cup is poisoned and, with her last breath, she tries to save her son by warning him:

> No, no, the drink, the drink,—O my dear Hamlet,—
> The drink, the drink!—I am poison'd.[3]

Laertes, himself being at death's door, then confesses that the tip of his sword had been poisoned and blames the king. Hamlet, though shocked, does not lose his head and acts promptly. Now at last, he takes vengeance upon Claudius and stabs him.

As Hamlet lies dying, the sound of soldiers marching is heard and also the sound of shots being fired. Fortinbras, the young Prince of Norway, had invaded Denmark earlier in the play. This had been discussed earlier and Hamlet had seen the preparations for war before he had left for England. Though he is dying, Hamlet realizes that now it is Fortinbras, who is a good noble prince, who will become the King of Denmark and asks Horatio to convey his best wishes to him. He dies before Fortinbras enters, leaving Horatio to vindicate him.

Fortinbras thus enters on a stage strewn with corpses and accords Hamlet the burial of a soldier. He is a man capable of taking right and quick decisions and Shakespeare gives the impression, as is usual at the end of Elizabethan tragedies, of moral order being restored and of ordinary life being recommenced through him:

For me, with sorrow I embrace my fortune:
I have some right of memory in this kingdom,
Which now to claim my vantage doth invite me.
... ...
Take up the bodies: such a sight as this
Becomes the field, but here shows much amiss.[4]

(b) The Genre of the Play

As it is, *Hamlet*, along with *Othello*, *King Lear* and *Macbeth*, is definitely categorized as one of the four Great Tragedies, yet there is difference of opinion about the kind of tragedy it is. First of all, in spite of many different views, it has to be conceded that it is basically a revenge tragedy. The Elizabethan Tragedy of Blood is divided into four categories (as has already been pointed out in *Introduction*, *supra*) and the revenge tragedy was one of the most popular ones. It was popularized in England by Kyd in his famous *The Spanish Tragedy*. The many different features of this kind of tragedy and their presence in *Hamlet* shall now be pointed out, since this is the prevailing view among critics.

(i) *A revenge tragedy*

Elizabethan revenge tragedy was mainly the result of the influence of Seneca and the phenomenal success of Kyd's play mentioned above. Many revenge tragedies were written in the next two decades and the genre itself underwent many modifications and developments. Though *Hamlet* was written more than a decade later, it resembles Kyd's play in many different ways.

The revenge tragedy has revenge as its central theme. The hero (and, sometimes, other characters as well) is motivated to avenge some wrong done to him or to someone dear to him. In Kyd, the hero's son is killed. He is also the betrothed of Bellimperia, so both the father Hieronymo and the beloved are motivated for wreaking vengeance. Here the question of morality comes in, for the act of vengeance, is forbidden by Christianity:

Recompense to no man evil for evil...

Dearly beloved, avenge not yourselves, but rather give place unto wrath: for it is written:

> Vengeance is mine; I will repay, saith the Lord.[5]

But, in order to generate pity and terror in the audience, the revenge has to be justified, and this is done in various ways thus:

> The Revenger of the drama started with the sympathy of the audience if his cause were good and if he acted according to the typical English notion of straightforward fair play.[6]

Thus, because the Ghost enjoins on Hamlet the act of revenge upon Claudius as a sacred and strictly filial duty, he has the sympathy of the audience also.

Revenge thus is the main action of such a play and all the events lead up to it. All the intrigues and episodes are brought in with this one and all-important aim in view. Extraneous actions have to be kept to a minimum and everything has to pertain to this objective:

> The audience is chiefly interested in the events which lead to the necessary revenge and then in the revenger's action in accordance with his vow.[7]

In order to avenge himself, the revenger makes use of several devices and these became the regular features of revenge tragedies. There is the ghost who urges revenge, hesitation or doubt on the part of the revenger, delay in the actual revenge, the real or the pretended madness of the revenger, the use of the inset play either to wreak revenge or to confirm the guilt of the wrong-doer. Along with these main features, there is also the use of highly rhetorical language, and a few other minor characteristics.

The delay in the revenge which is, after all, a dramatic necessity, is a point which needs great nicety on the part of the dramatist. It has to be dramatically justified and has to be brought about in such a way as not to imperil the hero with the imputation of cowardice or of Machiavellianism. What happens in *Hamlet* is thus fully in accord with the convention of revenge tragedy, though his endless hesitation has been understood in many different ways.

A significant fact about the revenge tragedy is that the hero himself does not create the circumstances that call for revenge—the situation is thrown upon him:

> The essence of any tragedy of revenge is that its hero has not created the situation in which he finds himself and out of which the tragedy arises.[8]

Thus in *Hamlet* we see the act of revenge upon Claudius being enjoined as a sacred duty by the Ghost of Hamlet's father:

> *Ghost*: List, list, O, list!
> If thou did ever thy dear father love,—
>
> *Hamlet*: O God!
>
> *Ghost*: Revenge his foul and most unnatural murder.[9]

So, Hamlet finds himself placed in a terrifying situation. He has to avenge his father's murder and betrayal, whether he wants or not. The Ghost appears to him again when he is talking to his mother to spur him into action. No wonder Hamlet cries out in agony:

> The time is out of joint: O cursed spite
> That ever I was born to set it right![10]

Again, the ultimate chance for the act of revenge is provided, in a paradoxical manner, by the villain himself. The wrong-doer manipulates events, all unconsciously, in such a way as to provide the revenger with just the chance he needs:

> The revenger takes an opportunity unconsciously provided for him by the villain. Given this opportunity which he seems unable to create for himself, he forms his schemes on the spur of the moment.[11]

In *Hamlet* also, the circumstances in which Hamlet finally takes vengeance upon Claudius are provided by Claudius himself. First of all, the occasion for the staging of *The Murder of Gonzago* is provided by him. It is he who tells Rosencrantz and Guildenstern "to draw him on to pleasure", which probably refers to dramatic performances. Concerning this, it had already been observed by Verity that "Claudius lays the trap for himself". Then the duel between Hamlet and Laertes is arranged by Claudius and the poisoned cup is also provided by him. Hamlet, all unwittingly wounds Laertes with the envenomed rapier. When he sees his mother die by drinking the poisoned cup and is told about the poisoned rapier he takes quick and inevitable action by running Claudius through as well as forcing him to drink his own poison. Not only did Claudius provide the opportunity for him, he even arranged the manner of his own death.

The play not only contains the usual ingredients of revenge tragedies but refines upon them in such a way that it becomes far more than a mere revenge tragedy. It raises questions on morality, psychology as well as dramaturgy that have continued to puzzle the reader even after four centuries. There are some critics, for example, who refuse to regard the play as a revenge tragedy at all:

> We may be told, in *Hamlet* Shakespeare is using the conventions of the revenge play.... This has always seemed to me a very rum argument indeed.[12]

He argues that it is very doubtful whether the Ghost is really the Ghost of Hamlet's father. It must be borne in mind that Hamlet too entertains such doubts. L.C. Knights is of the opinion that whether Hamlet believes in the authenticity of the ghost does not really matter, for when he accepts the injunctions laid upon him, he is doing so because he actually wants to kill Claudius. The Ghost offers him good reasons for yielding to the temptation. Not everyone will agree with this view.

The act of killing Claudius, again, has not been called an act of vengeance by G. Wilson Knight. He too refuses to look upon the play as a revenge tragedy and call the killing of Claudius "creative assassination":

> At the end, fate steps in, forces him to perform the act of creative assassination he has been, by nature of his inner disintegration, unable to perform.[13]

This is a highly individualistic view and it is very doubtful whether anyone will call an act of pre-meditated and long-drawn-out vengeance "creative". It is the duty of the diligent student however, to pay attention to all kinds of opinions, specially where an eminent and creative critic like G. Wilson Knight is concerned.

(ii) *A study of passions*

According to the German critic L.L. Schücking, *Hamlet* is a play of powerful "internal movement". This internal movement comprises the emotional upheaval in the characters' minds. The character themselves, because of their capacity for deep as well as intense emotions, are changing continually. This is the case with each character, not just the hero. Hamlet himself fluctuates from sombre melancholy in the beginning to a horrified realization of his duty in the Ghost scene. He is in a nearly frenzied condition in the scene reported by Ophelia who had been thoroughly frightened:

> Pale as his shirt, his knees knocking each other;
> And with a look so piteous in purport
> As if he had been loosed out of hell
> To speak of horrors,—he comes before me.[14]

This scene had taken place very soon after he had met the Ghost. He was in the throes of melancholy, contemplating suicide, just before the nunnery-scene in which he showed a cruelty and callousness so unnatural to him that Ophelia was convinced of his madness. After the performance of the inset play, he was in a state of elation at having caught Claudius at a disadvantage and in the closet-scene again he was so perturbed that the Queen was afraid of her own son and had cried out for help.

In the graveyard-scene however, at first, he is in a contemplative mood and then becomes frenzied, leaping into the grave and struggling with Laertes. There are very few scenes in which he behaves in a cool and collected manner.

The other characters also live an intensely active inner life. Ophelia, who is a passive and obedient girl undergoes a veritable purgatory of self-blame and becomes mad. The Queen, at first, is in an equable mood, though worried for her son. This equanimity is destroyed in the closet scene: "O Hamlet, thou hast cleft my heart in twain"[15] she cries out. King Claudius, showing himself to be a calm and collected administrator, is subjected to serious alarm and penitence after the staging of *The Murder of Gonzago*. Thereafter, his peace of mind is totally destroyed and he descends to ignoble and bloody stratagems to get rid of his stepson.

Schücking points out that such emotional upheavals are but normal in a tragedy. What marks Hamlet out is the intensity of them:

> Here it is the tempo, forced to the uttermost, that is so characteristic.[16]

He explains that in the play, emotions are presented not as mere emotion but as being so strong as to overwhelm the characters. In other words, emotions are swinging a character to extremes. The tragedy therefore is a study in different kinds of passions. He comes to the conclusion:

> *Hamlet* resembles other great Shakespeare tragedies in that it cannot be comprehended except as a study of passions.[17]

(iii) *Tragedy of reflection*

This is a very popular view and the phrase has been attributed to the play by A.C. Bradley according to the views of Schlegel and Coleridge. Both of these critics lay stress upon the powerful intellect of Hamlet, which makes him lean more towards reflection and contemplation than towards action. This contemplative cast of his mind gives birth to irresolution and hesitation in a very natural manner, for here, great moral issues are at stake:

> Here we see a great, an almost enormous intellectual activity, and a proportionate aversion to real action, consequent upon it, with all its sympathetic and accompanying qualities.[18]

This intellectual cast of Hamlet's mind is apparent from the very beginning of the play. He is already thinking of death in the first soliloquy itself, for the thought of his mother's marriage within two months of his father's death is a torture to his soul. All the time it is quite clear that he thinks too much and too long over everything. In the typical manner of an intellectual, he leaps from the particular to the general. Just because his mother has remarried (which after all is no out of the way occurrence, particularly in the case of reigning princes), the whole world becomes an unweeded garden. The Ghost tells him to avenge his murder and this terrible injunction is made to spring to the thoroughly abstract concept of time itself:

> The time is out of joint; O cursed spite
> That ever I was born to set it right![19]

His mother has betrayed her dead husband, as he thinks, by marrying again and therefore he blames womankind itself: "Frailty, thy name is woman". This trait of generalizing from particular instances, which is a direct result of his intellectual superiority, is to be seen throughout the play and most of all in his lack of resolution.

The tendency to ponder over every thought and action is seen the best in the soliloquies, particularly in the "To be or not to be" soliloquy. A detailed reading of this soliloquy will show not only Hamlet's habit of scrutinizing everything in detail, but how one thought inevitably leads to another thought which has to be scrutinized again. For example, he starts by pondering over the ethical and social significance of an active life ("to take up arms against a sea of troubles") and a contemplative one ("nobler in the mind to suffer"). Dying is, from time immemorial, associated with sleep and therefore, he next starts thinking about sleep. Thus, step by step, his analysis goes on in a manner typical of an intellectual. These are but the first few lines of only one soliloquy. Everywhere, throughout the play, his reactions are those of an intellectual. It is not at all surprising that no one, Polonius, Ophelia or Gertrude, can understand him—they all lack the analytical and critical detachment of the mind of an intellectual.

A.C. Bradley has called this the Schlegel-Coleridge theory of Hamlet's character and, as he has pointed out with great critical acumen:

> According to this, *Hamlet* is the tragedy of reflection. The cause of the hero's delay is irresolution; and the

> cause of this irresolution is excess of the reflective or speculative habit of mind.[20]

(iv) *Tragedy of moral idealism*

A.C. Bradley himself, partially agreeing with the above theory, calls *Hamlet* a tragedy of moral idealism. He analyzes Hamlet's character with these two traits in mind: (i) Hamlet's moral sensitivity and (ii) his idealism. He points out that the young Hamlet of the early part of the play has an extremely delicate sense of justice:

> We cannot be mistaken in attributing to the Hamlet of earlier days an exquisite sensitivity, to which we may give the name "morality".[21]

It is this morality that is outraged at every stage in the play. At first he thinks of his mother's unfaithfulness to his father's memory, then he comes to know that his uncle has murdered his father. Ophelia does not have the courage of love and returns his letters and gifts. Rosencrantz and Guildenstern carry his death-warrant though they are his school-fellows. It must be remembered that he thinks both of them know what is there in Claudius's letter, though there is no reason for thinking so. Indeed, one would not expect a man as crafty as Claudius to confide in these two men, but Hamlet thinks so. Thus, at every step, knowledge of the world's knavery and treachery continues to assail his sense of morality, till he is at the point of losing his reason. This would not have happened had he been a little less sensitive and a little more conversant with the way of the world. This sense, as Bradley holds, goes hand in hand with idealism—the two are actually in his mind, only to find corruption, stupidity and treachery everywhere. No wonder he feels contempt and an unavoidable derision. Bradley gives a list:

> ...Hamlet's disgust at his uncle's drunkenness, his mother's sensuality, his astonishment and horror at her shallowness, his contempt for everything merely external.[22]

The gradual but inevitable destruction of this moral idealism is seen in the events of the plot. Yet, in spite of all the horrors heaped upon him, Hamlet's idealism is so high and clear in his mind that he cannot bring himself to kill Claudius when he is at prayer and has to look for excuses to spare him:

> ...and am I then revenged, to take him in the purging of his soul, when he is fit and seasoned for his passage? No.[23]

many critics think this excuse to be a flimsy one. According to the present view, it is his moral idealism that stops his hand and A.C. Bradley has declared:

> *Hamlet* deserves the title "tragedy of moral idealism" quite as much as the title "tragedy of reflection".[24]

(v) *Religious drama*

A.C. Bradley had declared in 1904 that *Hamlet* cannot be called a religious drama in the specific sense, and, half a century later, H.D.F. Kitto the great classical scholar called it a religious drama, though not in any specific sense:

> What we are dealing with is no individual tragedy of character, however profound, but something more like religious drama.[25]

It should be borne in mind that in this context, the word "religious" does not refer to any specific religion like Christianity or pagan Greek religion, though Kitto draws parallels between *Hamlet* and the classical tragedies. He takes a far higher and wider view—concerning sin and punishment, repentance and redemption—that are part, not of just one specific religion, but of human life itself:

> we may say that both in the Greek trilogy[26] and in Shakespeare's play, the Tragic Hero, ultimately, is humanity itself, and what humanity is suffering from, in *Hamlet*, is not a specific evil, but Evil itself.[27]

Hamlet, indeed, can stand comparison with the best classical tragedies. According to Kitto, then, Shakespeare is concerned, not with the crime of just one person and the punishment meted out to him by another, but with the "corroding power of sin". This highly metaphysical interpretation of the play is supported in full by the events and, indeed, offers a most satisfactory solution to the many puzzles offered by it. Hamlet's soliloquies can be understood the best in the light of this view. His habit of generalization falls into the right perspective as well:

> Fie on't! O, fie! 'tis an unweeded garden,
> That grows to seed; things rank and gross in nature
> Possess it merely.[28]

This indeed, is a vision of Evil itself, spread over the whole world, not confined to one person. One of the important points, for example, as offered by this critic, is the manner in which evil also spreads itself from one soul to another. Laertes is tempted by Claudius, Polonius's stupid spying rouses murderous fury in Hamlet, Ophelia's innocence is corrupted into madness, Hamlet, infuriated by the death-warrant entrusted to his two friends sends them pitilessly to death.

Not all critics, however, agree with Kitto's approach to the vexed question of morality in this play. Though the story of the play belongs to pre-Christian times, Shakespeare himself has set it against a Christian background, and this has made us apply concepts of Christian ethics to it. Critics have pointed out that though Hamlet himself shows scruples over the act of suicide, he does not show any religious scruples over the act of vengeance itself. Observing this, Patrick Cruttwell asks:

> ...is it not strange that there should be none? For both play and character are notably Christian.[29]

He goes on to argue that the concept of revenge is, really speaking, never pitted against the ideas of Christian morality. According to him, this undermines the moral effect of the play and he finds it to be ambivalent in comparison with Kyd's play:

> It is this which makes the moral effect so much more ambiguous than that of a play which is revenge-play and nothing else, such as *The Spanish Tragedy*.[30]

Then Cruttwell refers to Kitto. He questions the term "religious drama" as applied by Kitto and points out that such terms can be applied only to such work as those in which the moral ambience is never in doubt. He comes to the conclusion:

> Such words would apply only to drama where the religious basis was clear cut and single; but what we have in *Hamlet* is an extraordinary muddle of two

> moralities, one avowed, the other not avowed, but both playing heavily and continuously on the central character.[31]

In spite of such refutations, Kitto's essay remains a very valuable one and offers comparison between Greek tragedy and *Hamlet*. The diligent student will also learn about the basic difference between Greek tragic thought and that of Shakespeare in this thought-provoking essay.

Apart from the views given above, *Hamlet* has been interpreted in many different ways. It has been called a "dramatic essay in mystery" by John Dover Wilson, "a tragedy of inaction" by Harley Granville-Barker, "a drama not of excessive thought but of defeated thought", a "drama of political crime" and many others. This multiplicity of interpretations serves to highlight the richness and complexity of the play.

NOTES

1. A.W. Verity, ed., *Hamlet*, Act II, sc. ii, ll.566-70, p. 56. Cambridge. The syndics of Cambridge Press, Indian edition, 1989. All further quotations from the text will be from this edition.
2. Act IV, sc. v, ll. 59-60, p. 99.
3. Act V, sc. ii, ll. 297-98. p. 133.
4. Act V, sc. ii. ll. 376-78...389-90, p. 136.
5. St. Paul's Epistle to the Romans, Chap. 12, verses 17-19. *The Holy Bible*. New York, American Bible Society, no date, p. 166.
6. F.T. Bowers, *Elizabethan Revenge Tragedy*, Princeton, Princeton Univ. Press, 1940, p. 40.
7. *Ibid.*, p. 63.
8. Helen Gardner, "The Historical Approach to Hamlet" in John Jump (ed.), *Hamlet: A Casebook*, Houndmills, Palgrave, 1968, p. 141.
9. Act I, sc. v, ll. 22-25, p. 27.
10. Act I, sc. v, ll. 189-90, p. 33.
11. Gardner, *op. cit.*, p. 142.
12. L.C. Knights, *An Approach to Hamlet*. London, Chatto and Windus, 1960, pp. 45-46.
13. G. Wilson Knight, *The Wheel of Fire*, London, Methuen and Co., 1977 rpt., p. 45.
14. Act II, sc. i, ll. 75-78, p. 36.

15. Act III, sc. iv, l. 155, p. 87.
16. John Jump, *op. cit.*, p. 43.
17. *Ibid.*
18. *Ibid.*, p. 30.
19. Act I, sc. v, ll. 189-90, p. 33.
20. A.C. Bradley, *Shakespearean Tragedy*, London, Macmillan and Co. Ltd., 1960, p. 83.
21. *Ibid.*, p. 88.
22. *Ibid.*, p. 89.
23. Act III, sc. iii, ll. 84-87, pp. 80-81.
24. Bradley, *op. cit.*, p. 90.
25. H.D.F. Kitto, *Hamlet as Religious Drama* in Jump, *op. cit.*, p. 108.
26. He is referring to the only complete Greek trilogy extant, Aeschylus's *Oresteia*, comprising *Agamemnon*, *Choephori* and *The Eumenides*—Author's note.
27. *Ibid.*, p. 114.
28. Act I, sc. ii, ll. 135-37, p. 14.
29. Patrick Cruttwell, *The Morality of Hamlet*, in Jump, *op. cit.*, p. 186.
30. *Ibid.*
31. *Ibid.*

4

A Scene-wise Analysis

Act I, sc. i

Like many other first scenes of Shakespeare's plays, this scene too sets the tone and creates the atmosphere of the play most effectively. It is located just in front of the castle at Elsinore and the time is midnight. Francisco is on sentry duty and is relieved by Bernardo. Horatio and Marcellus join them and Bernardo tells the former how for two successive nights he and Marcellus have seen the Ghost of the former king (whose name was also Hamlet). Horatio is sceptical and while they are talking the Ghost appears. Horatio exhorts it to speak, but it doesn't answer him and vanishes.

Horatio is now completely convinced of the reality of the Ghost and all of them fall to discussing the significance of its appearance. They all think that its appearance denotes some misfortune that is going to fall on the kingdom. Horatio, in an expository speech, tells the two officers how the elder Hamlet had killed Fortinbras the King of Norway in single combat. This victory had far-reaching consequences because the Norwegian king's lands then become the property of the elder Hamlet, that is, of Denmark. Now young Prince Fortinbras has attacked Denmark in order to avenge his father's death. Horatio is of the opinion that the Ghost has come to warn them of this, to help the kingdom.

The Ghost appears again and Horatio repeatedly adjures it to speak but the cock crows and it vanishes. Horatio then decide to acquaint Hamlet with this event, rightly judging that the Ghost wants to speak to him, not to them. With this, the scene comes to its close.

Elizabethan plays were written in a mixture of poetry and prose and many scenes use both. This scene however is entirely in blank verse and this blank verse, in the beginning, is so flexible that it sounds like natural conversation:

> The first twenty-two lines are built of the simplest words in the most homely idiom. Shakespeare had worked for a long time in the theatre, and written a good many plays, before reaching the point at which he could write those twenty-two lines.[1]

As Eliot had also pointed out, there is great variety in the blank verse used as well, for these first few lines are expository speech by Horatio which, in turn is different from the way he adjures the Ghost, in thirteen lines, to speak to him. There are several techniques for bringing about variations in blank verse (*vide* ch. 11, *infra*) that Shakespeare has used here.

Shakespeare's scenes are never isolated from the main body of the play—they are always linked to the foregoing and the ensuing scenes, so that the entire play might present a closely-woven appearance. This being the opening scene, is naturally not linked to any foregoing scene, but it looks forward to the next, in which Horatio tells Hamlet about the Ghost. As a matter of fact, the first appearance of the Ghost in this scene sows the seed for the action of the entire play, though some critics would give the credit for this to sc. iv of this Act, in which the Ghost tells Hamlet of his murder (*vide* ch. 12, *infra*). This scene, it cannot be denied, anticipates in many other ways the later events of the play and, most important of all, creates the atmosphere of tension and horror that is so typical of Elizabethan tragedies. This had been pointed out by Coleridge who, naturally, responded to the overtones of supernatural mystery and horror in the scene and had observed:

> ...the armour, the dead silence, the watchfulness that first interrupts it, the welcome relief of the guard, the cold...all excellently accords with, and prepares for, the afterwards gradual rise into tragedy.[2]

The scene, indeed, is highly complex. Not only does it, like a Prologue, acquaint the audience with what had happened in the past, but also anticipates later action. There is no clumsiness in the expository speeches of Horatio, because the two other officers are puzzled by the appearance of the Ghost and ask him for an explanation. Preparations are made for the appearance of the hero in a very quiet manner (Horatio refers to him as just "young Hamlet"). Coleridge had drawn attention to this quiet but effective mode of introducing the hero. The scene, thus, is highly functional, as, indeed, it has to be.

Analysing the impact of the opening scenes of Elizabethan tragedies, Una Ellis-Fermor isolates a few of Shakespeare's, Hamlet's among them, to point out that they show a departure from his usual method. He chooses a passage which may not take the action forward, but which sets the tone:

> In *Hamlet*, he sets the mood of apprehension and uneasiness by the appearance of the Ghost and the response of the characters to it, then introducing, very plausibly, a prologue speech in Horatio's reply to Marcellus.[3]

As an opening scene, this can hardly be bettered. It creates a mood of apprehension as well as expectation in the reader.

Act I, sc. ii

The second scene introduces us to the major characters of the play. It opens with a dignified speech by King Claudius in which he tells the assembled courtiers that after the death of the elder Hamlet he, Claudius, after a decent interval of mourning, has married the widow Queen and is now about to take up the governance of the realm. Young Fortinbras, eager to avenge the death of is father, has invaded Denmark and is importuning the king to return the lands won in fair combat by the dead king. Claudius sends an embassage to the old and decrepit uncle of Fortinbras, who is the present king of Norway. Claudius thinks that perhaps he is quite unaware of his nephew's doings and will have to be informed of them. He gives the two ambassadors Cornelius and Voltimand, clear instructions about their duties and powers. Claudius is thus shown to be a good and efficient king, conscious of his duties and knowledgeable about his neighbours. G. Wilson Knight draws attention to this fact:

> We see the government of Denmark working smoothly. Claudius shows every sign of being an excellent diplomatist and king.[4]

After having finished with the two ambassadors, Claudius turns to Laertes, asking him what he wants. Laertes merely wants permission to go back to France whence he had come to attend the coronation. After speaking graciously to him Claudius next turns to Hamlet—his nephew and now his stepson.

At once, there is a subtle but noticeable change of tone. Hamlet is hostile to his uncle, though this hostility is not yet apparent. At most, it manifests itself in his asides and in his refusal to cast off mourning. Both Claudius and the Queen request him to take off his mourning and then plead with him not to go back to the University of Wittenberg but to stay at Elsinore. Hamlet agrees to this and Claudius is truly delighted—so much so that he proposes to fire a volley from the canons in token of it.

Hamlet is then left alone and the first of his famous soliloquies is delivered. He is so resentful of and disgusted with his mother's marriage to his uncle and his accession to the throne that he thinks of dying. He talks most unkindly of his mother's remarriage within two months of his father's death in what he taken to be indecent haste:

> O God, a beast that wants discourse
> Would have mourn'd longer-married with my uncle.[5]

He is so bitterly disillusioned that the entire world seems to be poisoned to him and disgust at his mother spreads to entire womankind. Then Horatio enters with the two officers. From their conversation it becomes clear that Horatio has but recently come from Wittenberg and that he is a fellow-student whom Hamlet has not seen for quite some time. Then Horatio tells him about the Ghost. Hamlet cross-questions them quite rigorously and it is clear that he believes them, for after they leave the stage he exclaims:

My father's spirit in arms! all is not well;
I doubt some foul play: would the night were come![6]

This scene, like the previous one, is entirely in verse, and, in accordance with the rules of dramatic speech, the versification and diction varies according to the speaker and the occasion. The king in his opening speech, for example, speaks in formal language and slow rhythm, in measured and smooth-flowing lines. The rhythm changes in the slow and tortured soliloquy. In the passage where Hamlet cross-questions Marcellus, Bernardo and Horatio, however, the blank verse moves like lightning with the quick thrust and parry of the questions and their answers.

This scene looks back to the foregoing scene in various ways. The reference to young Fortinbras is one such link, for Horatio had talked about him in the former scene. Again, Horatio had also mentioned that they would tell Hamlet about the Ghost and here they do so. The scene looks forward to the fourth scene of this Act in that here Hamlet decides that he will accompany them in their watch that night in order to meet the Ghost and in the fourth scene the meeting does take place. This is characteristic of the way our dramatist proceeds—each scene is linked to the foregoing and the ensuing ones.

This is a long scene, containing 257 lines. Scenes of such length are usually divisible into two or more parts. This particular scene falls easily into three. The first 128 lines make up the first part of the scene in which Claudius, the Queen and the others are all present. Then they all leave the stage and this part of the scene ends. The second part is very short, consisting only of Hamlet's soliloquy ("O, that this too, too solid flesh would melt") till line 158. The third part of the scene begins with the entrance of Horatio and the two officers and constitutes the rest of the scene. It can be seen that the scene has thus a careful construction, with the soliloquy holding the central position, as it alone comprises the short but highly important middle section, flanked by two parts of almost equal length balancing each other. It is also important because most of the important characters are introduced in it. The only major character who still remains to be introduced is Ophelia who will come in the next scene.

Act I, sc. iii

This scene offers us better acquaintance with the Polonius family. Laertes is bidding farewell to his father and sister. He cautions Ophelia against Hamlet's advances to her, telling her not to take him seriously. He does not accuse Hamlet of insincere flirtation—far from it indeed:

> Perhaps he loves you now,
> And now no soil nor cautel doth besmirch
> The virtue of his will: but you must fear,
> His greatness weigh'd, his will is not his own.[7]

Ophelia, in her turn, tells him to be prudent in his own sphere and then Polonius enters. He blesses his son and delivers a speech full of sound advice. Such speeches are known as set-speeches, and are to be found in many plays. There are many kinds of set-speeches and the advice given by an older man (father, uncle, teacher, etc.) to a young man is a well-known one.

Polonius then asks Ophelia what Laertes has told her and Ophelia tells him about Hamlet's attentions. Polonius pooh-poohs the whole thing, making it quite clear that he does not think Hamlet to be at all serious in his protestations of love and tells her to discourage him.

The scene is entirely in verse and contains many memorable lines. Many lines in Polonius's speech have the force of proverbs:

> Give thy thoughts no tongue
> Nor any unproportion'd thought his act.
> Be thou familiar but by no means vulgar.
> ... .
> Give every man thy ear, but few thy voice:
> ... .
> For the apparel oft proclaims the man;
> ....
> Neither a borrower nor a lender be:

For loan oft loses both itself and friend,
... ...
This above all: to thine own self be true.[8]

Polonius is despised by Hamlet and treated by the critics as a more or less comic character, but the precepts he lays down are solid ones.

This scene is important in that it introduces Ophelia. Though the play does not contain a forceful heroine, yet this title has to be given to Ophelia. She is present in but a very few scenes and influences the action more after her death than before it. The scene is linked to the preceding one in that the former one mentions Laertes's departure for France. It anticipates the later scene in which Ophelia tells Polonius about Hamlet's frenzied behaviour.

Act I, sc. iv

This scene takes us once more to the same location and the same time of midnight (though twenty-four hours later) as the first scene. Hamlet, Horatio and Marcellus are up on the platform before the castle waiting for the Ghost. They hear the sounds of revelry as Claudius carouses in the castle and Hamlet expresses his disgust. This conversation which in itself is not important has been commented upon by Coleridge as being evidence of "Shakespeare's minute knowledge of human nature". He points out that often, while waiting for some important, taxing event, men turn to less important, ordinary things to lessen the pressure on their minds.

Before long, the Ghost appears and Hamlet, though alarmed at first ("Angels and ministers of grace defend us") addresses it as his father and implores it to speak. The Ghost beckons him to follow him and though Horatio and Marcellus try to deter him Hamlet shakes them off and goes out with the Ghost. Marcellus ulter the memorable line "Something is rotten in the state of Denmark" and the scene comes to its end.

This is a very short scene entirely in verse. It is linked to scene ii of this Act because in that scene, Hamlet had decided to meet the Ghost and here we see the outcome of that decision. It also creates suspense by looking forward to the next scene in which, the reader anticipates, the Ghost will reveal something of moment to Hamlet.

Act I, sc. v

This is a crucial scene because in it, the secret of the murder of the elder Hamlet is revealed by the Ghost. Even before telling Hamlet of the betrayal by Claudius, the Ghost lays upon Hamlet the duty of avenging him:

> *Ghost*: It thou didst ever thy dear father love,—
>
> *Hamlet*: O God!
>
> *Ghost*: Revenge his foul and most unnatural murder.[9]

The Ghost tells him how, as he lay sleeping in his orchard, Claudius had poured poison into his ears and he had died in agony. After killing him, Claudius not only took his throne but his wife as well. This kind of relationship was looked upon as incestuous at that time. Theodore Spencer says:

> Shakespeare's audience would remember that Henry VIII's marriage to Catharine of Aragon was proved illegal because it violated the law of Nature: it was incestuous because he had married, like Claudius, his brother's wife.[10]

It is noticeable that the Ghost still retains affection and consideration for his wife and does not blame her for marrying his treacherous brother. He adjures Hamlet again and again not to hurt the Queen:

> Taint not thy mind, nor let thy soul contrive
> Against thy mother aught: leave her to heav'n.[11]

Then, the Ghost vanishes, leaving Hamlet a prey to the most harrowing emotions. He takes his notebook out to take the whole thing down in writing. Then Horatio and Marcellus come in, eager to learn the outcome. Hamlet does not tell the secret to them, but makes them swear that they will never tell anyone about the Ghost. The Ghost, from under the earth, also commands them to swear. So they lay their hands on Hamlet's sword and swear never even to mention the incident. The scene ends with one of the best-known couplets of Shakespeare:

The time is out of joint: O cursed sprite,
That ever I was born to set it night.[12]

The scene is entirely in verse and contains a few couplets in addition to blanks verse. The most notable of these is the one quoted above. Such couplets, expressing an important idea in a terse and memorable, manner, are known as Seneca sentences for Seneca made extensive use of them. They are usually employed to point a moral, but our poet uses them for other purposes also, like summing up the thoughts and emotions of a person.

From the point of view of events and time, this scene immediately follows scene iv. It carries on where scene iv ends and is thus firmly linked to it. The future effect of the scene is immense, for the whole play, as a matter of fact, is the result of the Ghost's injunction upon Hamlet to avenge his murder. It is easily the most influential scene in the play. It anticipates later events in another way also, for here we get the first intimation that Hamlet is going to pretend to be mad. He tells Horatio:

As I, perchance, hereafter shall think meet
To put an antic disposition on.[13]

This hint shows the lightning-quick reactions of his mind. Only a few minutes have passed and he has already decided to feign madness. The reason thereof is not clear, but the fact that he is already thinking in these terms prepares the reader for the future. In spite of his saying clearly here as well as elsewhere that the madness is going to be a mere pretence, speculation has been rife among critics.

Uptil now, there has been no indication that the play might develop into a revenge tragedy, but after this scene there can be no doubt about it. So, this scene is the one that determines conclusively the genre of the play. Hamlet takes on the role of a revenger with great solemnity, making a ritual of it:

> The scene at the close of Act I sc. v is a deliberate self-dedication, made as conspicuously as possible, to the role of a revenger. Hamlet invents a brief ritual, a ceremony.[14]

This scene, like the second scene of this Act, is balanced equally on the two sides of a soliloquy. The first part of the scene, till line 90 with the exit of the Ghost is succeeded by a twenty-line soliloquy, to be followed by another 90 lines. One can say either that the scene is divided into two halves, joined by a soliloquy, or that it has three parts, with the soliloquy marking a short division by itself. This is exactly like the second scene in construction.

This is also the last scene of this Act. The first Act of Elizabethan plays usually introduces the main characters and begins the action. This function is carried out by this Act. All the important characters have been introduced, the proper ingredients of a revenge tragedy have been presented and the action has already begun with the Ghost's revelations. In addition, Shakespeare has introduced the element of Spectacle (*Opsis*) which, according to Aristotle is one of the basic elements of tragedy. This has been done by using the element of the supernatural in the character of the Ghost. It is not very often that this element is used thus early in a play. Two notable exceptions are Kyd's play in which the allegorical figures of Revenge and the Ghost of Andrea appearing in the very first scene, and Shakespeare's own Macbeth in which also the three witches are brought in the first scene. As yet, all the scenes have been in blank verse, with occasional use of Senecan couplets and we have not had the opportunity of sampling Shakespeare's dramatic prose as yet.

Act II, sc. i

The scene opens in the house of Polonius. He is sending his man Reynaldo to Paris to take Laertes, some money and papers. Polonius instructs this man to find out as much about Laertes's lifestyle in Paris as he can—in other words, to spy upon him.

After some time, Ophelia enters, in a distressed and frantic condition. Hamlet had visited her and had behaved in an extremely puzzling manner. He was disheveled and had acted in a frenzied way. Polonius at once draws the conclusion most natural to him—that he has gone mad out of disappointed love for her. She had, according to his instructions, repulsed him and

Polonius blames himself for being the unwitting cause for his madness. He hastens to Claudius with Ophelia, saying that the king must be told of this development.

This is not an important scene. The only important purpose it serves is to acquaint the reader with the fact that Hamlet has started to put his plans into action by feigning madness. This pretence has given rise to long and complex debates in the centuries that have followed, some critics are thinking that it is really a pretence, and some that it is not all pretence—that Hamlet is truly half distracted with grief, disgust and tension. Different critics, doctors and psychologists have each produced his own view. It must be remembered that pretended or real madness was a popular device used in revenge drama. Hieronymo in Kyd's *Spanish Tragedy* pretends to be mad. Moreover, Hamlet had already said in the last scene that he might "put an antic disposition on".

The scene is thus firmly linked to the preceding scene in two ways—the mention of Laertes in Paris, and Hamlet's madness, whether real or pretended. It also looks forward to the next scene in which Hamlet's lunacy seems to be a fact that is accepted by everyone. Though a short scene, it can be clearly divided into two parts, the second commencing with Ophelia's entrance.

Act II, sc. ii

This is the longest scene of the play, containing 583 lines, and is located in the castle. Claudius had sent for Rosencrantz and Guildenstern, who are both Hamlet's schoolmates, to come and kept him company. They are to entertain Hamlet and find out the cause of his mental disturbance. By this time, it has became clear that something is wrong with Hamlet and both, Claudius and the Queen are worried. They think that perhaps Hamlet will confide to his friends what he cannot bring himself to tell anyone else. Rosencrantz and Guildenstern agree to do all they can.

Then Polonius enters, bringing the news that Voltimand and Cornelius who had been sent to Norway (Act I, sc. ii.) have returned and also tells the king that he has found out "the very cause for Hamlet's lunacy". The two ambassadors are given audience first and they recount the success of their mission. Then Polonius presents his hypothesis to Claudius—that Ophelia's rejection has turned Hamlet mad. He shows the king and the Queen the letter Hamlet had written to Ophelia, professing deep love in the chivalric tradition. He also tells them how he had told his daughter to repulse Hamlet and that it is this that has caused the overturning of Hamlet's reason. They plan to verify this by eavesdropping on a meeting between Hamlet and the biddable Ophelia.

Then they see Hamlet coming and all of them except Polonius withdraw. There follows a dialogue between Hamlet and Polonius which serves to confirm Polonius's hypothesis. Then he leaves and Rosencrantz and Guildenstern enter. Hamlet welcomes them cordially but he has his suspicions that perhaps Claudius had called the two of them to spy on him. He puts his question quite frankly:

> Were you sent for? Is it your own inclining? Is it a free visitation? Come, deal justly with me.[15]

The two of them admit that Claudius had sent for them. Then there follows a splendid speech by Hamlet in which he first tells them that he is in a very disturbed frame of mind. He looks at the wonderful and sublime creation of God—the world, and it appears to him to be a "foul and pestilent congregation of vapours". He looks at man and though man is the most glorious creation Hamlet finds him to be a "quintessence of dust". The critical comments on this famous passage are truly numberless. G. Wilson knight, for example, has extensively commented on the punctuation in this passage on man.

Then Rosencrantz tells him that a troupe of players has arrived at court to offer entertainment. It should be noted that earlier in this scene Claudius had asked the two of them "to draw him on to pleasures". This is the pleasure or the entertainment that he has arranged for Hamlet and it will, paradoxically, give Hamlet the chance to put up the play that will prove his guilt. Verity observes:

> Claudius lays the trap for himself. He probably knows Hamlet's partiality for the drama.[16]

The observation that Helen Gardner makes on the chances that the villain offers to the hero for wreaking vengeance has already been mentioned (*vide* the section on revenge tragedy in Chapter IV, *supra*).

Hamlet gives the two schoolmates to understand that he is not really mad and that he can see through them. Then Polonius arrives once more, to tell him that the Players have arrived. In a dialogue with Polonius, Hamlet again refers to his daughter as he had done in the earlier one and this again confirms Polonius's hypothesis ("Still on my daughter").

Then the Players arrive and there follows the scene in which Hamlet discusses the art of dramatic performance. The First Player delivers a demonstration-speech which is actually in continuation with one that Hamlet has already declaimed. Then, on Hamlet's request he delivers another on Hecuba, on which Hamlet's comments (given later) have become famous. Then, isolating the First Player from the rest, he asks whether they have *The Murder of Gonzago* in their repertoire, and on being told that they have, requests them to insert a few lines into it which he will write himself. Then all go away, leaving Hamlet to deliver another of his famous soliloquies.

In this soliloquy, Hamlet starts by self-depreciation ("O what a rogue and peasant slave am I") goes on to reflect upon the performance of the Players and then comes back to himself, blaming himself for not having taken vengeance, as yet, upon Claudius. Finally, he expresses doubts about the authenticity of the Ghost and hopes that the play will take Claudius unawares and make him react in such a manner as to reveal his guilt:

> The play's the thing
> Wherein I'll catch the conscience of the king.[17]

This is not only the longest scene of the play but also the last scene of the second Act. It is written in a mixture of prose and verse. The dialogue is in blank verse up till line 170, when Hamlet arrives. All the dialogues with Hamlet are in prose, except for the speeches declaimed by Hamlet and the First

Player. After that, the dialogue is continued in prose and only when Hamlet is at last alone on the stage does he speak in blank verse. The use of prose is significant. Hamlet is pretending to be mad and madmen are usually given prose in Elizabethan drama—it is one of the contemporary stage-customs.

The scene is so long as to be almost shapeless. It can be divided into no less than seven parts, though it is open to discussion.

1. Lines 1-39 (*exeunt* Rosencrantz, etc.).
2. Line 40 (Polonius: "The ambassadors, etc.) to line 84 (*Exeunt* Voltimand and Cornelius).
3. Line 85 (Pol.: This business) to 170 (Enter Hamlet).
4. Line 171 (Enter Hamlet) to 216 (Hamlet: These tedious old fools, etc.).
5. Line 217 (Enter Rosencrantz) to 403 (Enter Players).
6. Line 404 (Ham.: You are welcome) to 524 (*Exeunt* Rosencrantz and Guildenstern).
7. Line 525 (Ham.: Now I am alone) to end.

This scene has a structure different from the ones already discussed. In many of the scenes, the different parts balance or equal each other. Here, the scene proceeds by different stages, each stage reaching a certain point of development and leading to the next. It begins at a slow tempo and gradually builds up to a climactic point in the oration on the dignity of man, and then gradually subsides, to rise high once more in the last soliloquy. It may seem that the pompous declamations of the First Player make up a high point, but it would be a wrong move to think so because all that bombast is not meant to be taken seriously.

As far as the action is concerned, we see that the main theme of the play—revenge—is taken a step further. We are also shown the success of the embassage to Norway which proves Claudius and Polonius think that they have a clue to Hamlet's madness. It is an eventful scene.

It is also integrally linked to the preceding and the following scenes. The return of the two ambassadors links it to Act I, sc. ii, Hamlet's feigned madness to both Act I, sc. v and to

Act II, sc. i. The Player-scene links it to Act III, sc. ii in which the inset play *The Murder of Gonzago* will be staged.

This is the last scene of this Act. It is a short Act, having only two scenes. Now the action is fairly under way and the tempo is becoming fast. Dramatic tension is being built up and the audience looks eagerly forward to see how Claudius is going to react to the inset play and what Hamlet is going to do thereafter.

Act III, sc. i

The scene shows Claudius questioning Rosencrantz and Guildenstern about Hamlet. The Queen, Polonius and Ophelia are also present on the stage. The two courtiers cannot tell anything except that Hamlet has not taken them into his confidence. He has only told them that he is in a highly disturbed state of mind. They also tell him about the play which is going to be performed that evening and Polonius confirms this, communicating Hamlet's invitation to them.

Now Claudius, Polonius and Ophelia are on the stage and they prepare to see how Hamlet is going to react to Ophelia's presence. So, Polonius gives Ophelia a book and the two of them withdraw.

Hamlet enters and delivers the famous soliloquy "To be or not to be". At first he does not see Ophelia and then, noticing her, speaks to her. She returns some love-tokens he had given her. It is a moving dialogue, for Hamlet is pretending to be mad and talks in a disjointed manner. He says, "I did love you once" and in the very next sentence tells her "I loved you not". G. Wilson Knight, taking it for granted that his mind is truly unhinged, says:

> Sick of the world, of man, of love, Hamlet denies the reality of his past romance: "I loved you not". This statement alone fits coherently into his diseased mind.[18]

Ophelia's reply to this bald and cruel statement is very revealing. She says quietly "I was the more deceived". She is a passive and quiet character and instead of blaming him takes the blame upon herself. It has been remarked that here

Shakespeare has worked more through implication than through direct statement:

> Here there is not only "the sickening drop from hope to despair" but the fineness of breeding that controls reproach.[19]

Ophelia's lament for what she thinks to be the total ruin of so fine a man is one of the most moving speeches delivered by her.

Then Claudius and Polonius enter and the former is sure that it is not love that is the cause of Hamlet's lunacy. He, with more sense than his minister, surmises a deep and hidden grief:

> There is something in his soul,
> O'er which his melancholy sits on brood.[20]

He is very uneasy about Hamlet and decides to send him to England and Polonius agrees with him, but asks him to wait and see if the Queen cannot get Hamlet to confide in her. The scene ends here.

This is a relatively unimportant one, but it contains what is perhaps the best known soliloquy of Hamlet—a soliloquy that has come to express contemporary man's (and that of modern man), spirit of world-weariness. This gives the scene a very special importance, though not as far as the action goes. Besides this the scene between Hamlet and Ophelia, known as the nunnery scene (and also as the eaves-dropping scene) is a significant one.

The scene is in a mixture of prose and verse, for Hamlet's dialogue with Ophelia is entirely in prose, as he is pretending to be mad. Besides blank verse, it contains two Senecan couplets in the customary way. One of these is spoken by Ophelia and the other by Claudius.

Like all the other scenes, this too is linked to the foregoing and the ensuing ones through the mention of the Players and the matter of Hamlet's love for Ophelia. Only one new development occurs—Claudius's decision to send Hamlet out of the country, to England.

Act III, sc. ii

This is the second longest scene in the play, comprising 382 lines. It is in this scene that the insert play is performed. At first, there is a dialogue between Hamlet and the First Player in which Hamlet directs him how to deliver the speech he has written. This entire dialogue is well-known for expressing Shakespeare's opinions about acting. He cautions the actor against over-acting:

> ...if you mouth it, as many of your players do, I had as life the town-crier spoke my lines. Nor do not saw the air too much with your hands.[21]

He tells them not to be too mild either, but to observe a proper mean, so that the acting neither offends by being too loud nor by being unnaturally soft but takes the middle way:

> Be not too tame neither, but let your own discretion be your tutor: suit the action to the word, to the action.[22]

Polonius, Rosencrantz and Guildenstern then enter and tell him that the King and the Queen are both coming to see the play. Hamlet then gets rid of all three of them and, calling Horatio, tells him to observe the king's reactions very carefully. He has already confided to Horatio the secret of his father's murder.

The court then enters. They all settle down, with Hamlet taking his place at Ophelia's feet and the play-within-the-play begins.

First, there is a dumb-show. The entire story of the elder Hamlet's death and Claudius winning the Queen is enacted. Neither the king nor the Queen react in any way (which has made critics think that perhaps they had been talking and not paid attention to the play at all). Then the Prologue enters. He, however departs from the customary Prologue in not saying anything about the play but withdraws after speaking three lines.

The Player king and the Player Queen then enter and the two profess their love for each other. The Player Queen, particularly, inveighs against second marriages. Then the Player king lies down to sleep, just as the elder Hamlet had done. At this point Claudius asks whether there is anything disagreeable in the play and Hamlet tells him there is nothing. This has made some critics think that perhaps he has not seen the dumb-show. Then he asks for the name and Hamlet tells him it is *The Mouse-trap*. The king, of course, does not realize that it is he who is the mouse being trapped.

Then Lucianus the Player king's nephew enters and pours the poison into the sleeping king's ears. This is too much for Claudius and he rises hastily and, calling for lights, goes away. The performance is stopped. Only Hamlet and Horatio are left on the stage.

Hamlet is so elated at this unequivocal proof of Claudius's guilt that he breaks out into a song. So is Horatio. The two friends talk excitedly, but not for long, because soon enough Rosencrantz and Guildenstern enter, to tell him that Claudius is extraordinarily perturbed and that the Queen wants to speak to him as soon as possible. Hamlet promises to go to her directly. Rosencrantz then appeals to Hamlet's good nature and, reminding him of the friendship they had, pleads with him to confide in him. Hamlet, however, refuses to do so, for he is quite sure that the two young men are no longer devoted to him:

> 'Sblood, do you think I am easier to be played on than
> a pipe? Call me what instrument you will, though you
> can fret me, you cannot play upon me.[23]

Then Polonius comes in, bringing the Queen's summons and there is a dialogue between him and Hamlet in which a courtier's sycophancy is mocked. Hamlet tells him to inform the Queen that he will soon meet her and they all go out, leaving him alone on the stage.

A short soliloquy follows. Hamlet is in the right mood for any deed of violence. First, however, he has to go and meet the Queen. He takes a firm resolution to speak roughly to her:

> Let me be cruel, not unnatural:
> I will speak daggers to her, but use none.[24]

The soliloquy ends with a Senecan couplet which brings the scene to an end.

This, the second longest scene in the play has been written in a mixture of prose and verse. More than three-fourths of the scene, in fact, is in prose. Hamlet speaks only twice in blank verse in his dialogue with Horatio (about 20 lines) and at the end (about 12 lines). Horatio speaks a few lines in verse and the rest of the scene, except for the play/let, is in prose. This is done in order to isolate the playlet from the rest of the scene. Two stanzas and a couplet of a song are also there. The versification as well as the language of the play-let, is stilted and bombastic as is but proper, for it is a stylised piece of work.

The most significant way in which the scene is linked to the preceding and the following ones is through the playlet. Actually, the connection goes farther back, to Act I, sc. v in which Hamlet says: "O good Horatio, I'll take the ghost's word for a thousand pounds" (I, v, 272-73), and, of course, has far-reaching repercussions in the later scenes.

The most important event that occurs is the performance of the playlet. Apart from confirming Claudius's guilt, it provides the element of spectacle (for more information see ch. 9, *infra*) and is also one of the characteristic features of the revenge tragedy.

Like the second scene of the second Act, this too, being a long scene, can be divided into several sections. These are roughly five:

Line 1 to Line 44 (Hamlet: Go make you ready).

Line 45 (Ham.: How now, my lord!) to L. 89 (Ham.: Get you a place).

L. 90 (Claudius: How fares our cousin) to L. 256 (All: Lights, lights, lights!).

L. 257 (Ham.: Why let the etc.) L. 370 (Ham.: Leave me, friends).

L. 371 (Ham.: 'Tis now, etc.) to end.

As in the scene mentioned above here also the different parts each follows the foregoing ones in a natural way but there is an attempt at balancing them or putting them in a pattern. The middle section of the scene is the one that contains the playlet and it is flanked on both sides by two rather unimportant sections in both of which Hamlet is the chief speaker. In the first two sections he speaks to the first Player and then to Horatio and in the following ones to the two courtiers and Polonius. The playlet, as is to be expected, occupies the central position. It is a very well-constructed scene and the playlet gives it a unique importance.

Act III, sc. iii

This can be held to be one of the two central scenes of the play. The text in use has twenty scenes in all, therefore there is no one central scene. This scene and the next are the two that come in the middle of the play (*vide* ch. 13, *infra*, comments on the text).

This scene continues the action immediately after the preceding one. Claudius confides his apprehensions and uneasiness to Rosencrantz and Guildenstern and tells them to prepare to accompany Hamlet to England.

After the two young men have left, Polonius comes to tell him that Hamlet is going to the Queen and he will hide behind the tapestry in her room to overhear their conversation. He assures Claudius that he will meet him later and tell him what had transpired in this meeting between mother and son. After he has gone there is a soliloquy by the king in which he expresses great remorse:

> O, my offence is rank, it smells to heaven;
> It hath the primal eldest curse upon 't,
> A brother's murder![25]

Torn by remorse, he kneels down to pray and this is the time when Hamlet enters. He is on his way to the Queen, and, seeing Claudius at prayer he realizes that he will never get a chance like this again. But then he starts reasoning it out. As Claudius is praying, his soul is in communication with God and it will go straight to heaven if he is killed now. Therefore, thinks Hamlet, it would be better to kill him when he would be in such a condition as not to merit salvation. So he sheathes his sword, thinking that since Claudius had, in killing his father, denied him salvation he deserves to be sent to hell.

This incident has received various interpretations. It has been thought to be downright wicked on Hamlet's part to deliberately postpone the act of revenge so that Claudius may be damned. It has also been thought that Hamlet is congenitally incapable of taking instant decisions or of killing anyone, so he makes use of a flimsy excuse to hide his inability. According to A.C. Bradley, who takes a positive view, Hamlet is far too noble a man to attack someone who cannot fight back:

> The incident of the sparing of the king is contrived with extraordinary dramatic insight.... One of his minor difficulties.... Probably was that he seemed to be required to attack a defenceless man; and here this difficulty is at its maximum.[26]

Hamlet goes on his way and Claudius rises. The prayer has been unseless for he himself realized that his heart had not been in it:

> My words fly up, my thoughts remain below;
> Words without thoughts never to heaven go.[27]

This short scene is entirely in verse and no notable events occur in it. But that which does not occur is important, namely, the act of revenge. The sparing of Claudius throws light on Hamlet's character, but does not take the action forward. The scene is in link with the foregoing one in point of time, for it immediately follows it, and looks forward to the next in which Hamlet will meet the Queen.

Act III, sc. iv

This is the famous closet-scene in which Hamlet harangues his mother. It also contains the last appearance of the Ghost.

The scene beings quietly enough, with a dialogue between the Queen and Polonius. He is ready for eavesdropping and quickly hides behind the tapestries. The Elizabethan stage, with curtains covering the three sides, afforded easy hiding places and this opportunity for providing dramatic irony is used in many plays. A celebrated example is to be found in Ben Jonson's *Volpone* in a scene in which Volpone the hero hides behind the curtains (known as arras also) and repeatedly sticks out his head thus providing comic laughter as well as dramatic irony. Here however, there is no laughter, for the device leads to Polonius's death.

From the very beginning, Hamlet takes an aggressive tone, accusing the Queen of having been unfaithful to her first husband, the elder Hamlet. The Queen is so alarmed by his rough behaviour (and it must be borne in mind that everybody, including herself believes him to be at least half-mad, if not fully so) that she cries out for help and so also does Polonius. Hamlet, thinking Claudius to be hiding there makes a thrust with his sword and kills Polonius instantly. When Hamlet lifts up the curtain and sees the dead body, he does not evince any shock or repentance and instead takes to haranguing the Queen.

He makes the Queen conscious of having done something shameful, if not criminal in marrying her brother-in-law. She becomes deeply repentant and asks him to stop:

> O speak to me no more
> These words, like daggers, enter in mine ear,
> No more, sweet Hamlet.[28]

Hamlet, however, means to go on and stops only when the Ghost interferes. He had told Hamlet not to harm the Queen and perhaps thinks that Hamlet has punished her enough. He tells Hamlet that he has come only to prod him on, and also tells him to take care of his mother. She cannot see or hear him and Hamlet's actions (looking at the Ghost and speaking to him) only confirms her belief in his madness.

The Ghost vanishes and Hamlet goes on with his plan of speaking daggers (Act III, sc. ii, l. 379) to the Queen till she cries out "O Hamlet, thou hast cleft my heart in twain". After speaking a few more lines Hamlet points to the dead body and says he repents this inadvertent act of violence. He also tells her quite clearly that he is not truly mad but only pretending to be so and also tells her his suspicions that Claudius, in sending him to England, means some mischieves, but that he himself is confident of his capacity to foil this plan. He then goes out, dragging Polonius's body to hide it in a nearby room.

This scene, as pointed out earlier, occurs in the middle of the play and together with the preceding one makes up the two central scenes of it. The only important event that takes place in it is the murder of Polonius, which will spark off the third revenge action of the play, that of Laertes seeking to avenge the death of his father. The scene also anticipates Hamlet's departure, for the murder of Polonius will hurry forward this event. It also makes us aware that he suspects Claudius of harbouring evil designs against him.

This scene is also important in that it contains the element of the special phenomenon of the supernatural, for the Ghost makes his final appearance in it. It is notable that he is perceived only by Hamlet. Horatio and the others had seen him but he had not spoken to them. They had heard his subterranean voice. In this scene the Queen neither sees nor hears him. It would definitely have been more dramatic if she had done so, but perhaps Shakespeare had wanted the audience to think that the Ghost does not manifest himself to her out of consideration—she might be very frightened on seeing him.

This is the last scene of this, the central Act. The entire Act thus contains four scenes and the action advances considerably. Hamlet has got the proof of Claudius's guilt and the motive for the third blood-revenge has also been introduced.

Act IV, sc. i

This scene takes place in a very short time after the last scene, if not immediately so. The King is perturbed on seeing the Queen in a very disturbed condition. On being questioned, she tells him how, in his madness, Hamlet has killed Polonius. Claudius, with great presence of mind, makes Rosencrantz and Guildenstern go at once in search of Hamlet and also of the dead body, and decides to send him away, out of the country, that very night. It is a short scene, entirely in verse, and serves as a link between the preceding scene and the next one.

Act IV, sc. ii

This is the shortest scene of the play, containing only thirty lines. Rosencrantz and Guildenstern ask Hamlet what he has done with the body of Polonius. Hamlet refuses to tell them and demands to be taken to the king. This too is a link-scene and takes place only a few minutes after the last one. Now that half of the play is done, the action is speeding up and these short scenes are an indication of that.

Act IV, sc. iii

The scene shows Rosencrantz telling Claudius that Hamlet has divulged the hiding place of Polonius's dead body. Then Hamlet enters with Guildenstern, and after some quibblings, tells them he had hidden it in the lobby.

Claudius then tells Hamlet that he must leave for England as soon as possible, and after he has left to prepare for the journey, sends for Rosencrantz and Guildenstern to follow him. Then in a soliloquy, he reveals his evil intentions. He is sending a sealed letter to the king of England, telling him to kill Hamlet. Rosencrantz and Guildenstern, it is to be guessed, do not know about the contents of this letter that they are to carry.

Referring to the dialogue between Hamlet and Claudius, G. Wilson knight observes that it serves to show the disorientation of Hamlet's mind:

> Even more horrible are his disgusting words about Polonius.... The horror of humanity doomed to death and decay has disintegrated Hamlet's mind.[29]

Wilson Knight is a critic who is convinced that Hamlet is at least half-mad, if not fully so. His analysis of the play, its theme, its structure and, above all the character of Hamlet, is coloured by this view (*vide* ch. VI & VII, *infra*)

Act IV, sc. iv

This is another short scene of 67 lines only. It is not exactly a link-scene like the three foregoing ones, i.e. scenes i, ii and iii of this Act, and Verity has used the term "side-scene" to describe it. Here a new character, Fortinbras, has been introduced. We have already been told about him in Act I, sc. i, by Horatio and later by Claudius as well, who had sent messengers to his uncle. Young Fortinbras provides, as has already been pointed out, the first action of blood-revenge in the play. Of the three revenge actions in the play, his is the least important, though it is introduced first.

The scene is chiefly remarkable for Hamlet's soliloquy beginning "How all occasions do inform against me". He sees Fortinbras training an army in order to take vengeance upon Denmark. As a matter of fact Fortinbras's desire for revenge is not to be justified, for his father was killed in fair fight, strictly in accordance with the rules of chivalry. Yet he thirsts for revenge and is up in arms. In comparison, Hamlet has done nothing. Instead he has got himself exiled from his country, at least for the time being. So he is full of self-blame for not having, as yet, avenged the death of his father. This speech is not included in all the editions, and, when the play is performed is usually omitted on the stage. This scene and the three foregoing ones, being short, all expedite the action.

Act IV, sc. v

This, after four short unimportant scenes, is again another important scene. It begins with the Queen refusing to see Ophelia, who has become mad. Horatio and a Gentleman persuade her to admit Ophelia to her presence. Horatio fetches her.

It is a very moving scene. Ophelia is entirely mad. She sings a song (which is an old ballad), in which there are moving references to a lover's death:

> He is dead and gone, lady,
> He is dead and gone;
> At his head a grass-green turf,
> At his heels a stone.[30]

There are some more stanzas. Finally she bids good-night to the ladies and goes out.

Claudius, as deeply moved as the Queen, gives orders that close watch be kept on her and, with a lot of insight, exclaims:

> O, this is the poison of deep grief; it springs
> All from her father's death.[31]

Now there is some noise off-stage and one of the courtiers enters to tell them how Laertes, having heard of Polonius's death, has come from Paris to take vengeance upon Claudius. He has mustered a crowd together which supports him. They have invaded the palace. Claudius, however, does not lose his head. Instead he quickly takes this opportunity to use Laertes's blood-thirstiness to turn him against Hamlet. Even while they are talking Ophelia comes in once more singing a ballad. She gives flowers to Claudius, the Queen and Laertes and perhaps to Horatio as well. This pathetic scene does but whet the keenness of Laertes's thirst for revenge and Claudius takes him aside to tell him the truth about Polonius death.

This scene, almost entirely in verse except for the two mad-scenes of Ophelia, is an eventful one. Ophelia's madness is shown, and Laertes's desire for revenge. It is a long scene and falls into four clear-cut divisions. The first section lasts till the speech of Claudius after the exit of mad Ophelia (L. 79). The second section begins with the entrance of the Gentleman bringing the news about Laertes and lasts till the second entrance of Ophelia (L. 137). The third section begins with Laertes's speech at the sight of Ophelia and lasts till her exit (L. 137-L. 181). Then the dialogue between the king and Laertes makes up the last section.

Ophelia's madness, her songs and gift of flowers have inspired many other mad-scenes in contemporary drama. As it is, madness, real or pretended is a common feature of revenge drama and *Hamlet* has both. Her speeches appear to be disjointed and nonsensical but are full of many implications. The flowers she gives all have multiple symbolic values. She herself explains these symbolisms and the Elizabethan audience, being already familiar with these deeper meanings, would have understood them. They become all the more significant as Ophelia gives them to different persons, pointing out the meaning in each case:

> There's rosemary, that's for remembrance; pray you, love, remember: and there is pansies, that's for thoughts.[32]

These are presumably given to Laertes, who later comments upon them. Likewise, she gives other flowers to the others. It should be remarked that she speaks in prose. As has been already pointed out with Hamlet's own supposedly mad speeches, mad persons were given prose by the dramatists of the time. Both of these short sequences, or scenes-within-scene, of Ophelia's madness will fall within the category of "pathetic scenes" as given by Aristotle.

Act IV, sc. vi

This is the second shortest scene of the play, comprising only 30 lines. Though short, it is a highly significant scene because it gives the information to Horatio that Hamlet's ship had been attacked by a pirate ship. He had boarded that ship while fighting them and they are holding him to ransom now. Hamlet has written a letter to the King to this effect and asks Horatio to accompany the sailor who has brought the letter and he will bring him (Horatio) to Hamlet. The letter also tells him that Hamlet's own ship, with Rosencrantz and Guildenstern in it, is on its way to England, and that he has a lot to tell Horatio about these two men.

The scene is mainly in prose for the letter from Hamlet which is in prose and which Horatio reads aloud constitutes the bulk of it. He himself speaks only five lines in verse. The scene acquaints us with the fact that Claudius's plan has miscarried and that Hamlet is unexpectedly coming back home.

Act IV, sc. vii

In this scene, at first, we see the King and Laertes conversing. Claudius has already told Laertes that it is Hamlet who killed Polonius, but that he had not been able to punish him properly because of the Queen, and his popularity in the kingdom. Before they can hatch any plan, however, a Messenger comes, bringing letters from Hamlet in which he announces that he is coming back.

Again, Claudius is quick to seize this opportunity. He tells Laertes that he will arrange a fencing-match between him and Hamlet and proposes that he kill Hamlet during it. Laertes further assures him that he will envenom the tip of his sword with a very strong poison so that if he can but lightly scratch Hamlet, he will surely die. To make things even more certain,

Claudius says that he will keep a cup of poisoned wine ready for Hamlet to refresh himself between the bouts in the duel so that Hamlet will die even if he escapes Laertes's sword.

No sooner have they hatched this diabolical plan, than the Queen enters. She brings the dreadful news that Ophelia has died by drowning. She had fallen in a river by the breaking of a branch of a tree on which she was lying. For a time, borne up by her dress, she floated in the water. As her clothes gradually got wet however, they dragged her down.

It has been suggested that the Queen's speech is something in the nature of an afterthought on the dramatist's part—Shakespeare attached this speech much later after the completion of the play. What the Queen's speech does not, and indeed cannot, clarify is whether the death is accidental or a suicide. This is left in doubt and we are later told that the Church is also in doubt about the precise nature of her death. The speech describing the nature of her death is one of the most beautiful set speeches in Shakespeare and has inspired poets and painters alike. Thus, after describing the tree and the brook, the Queen goes on:

> An envious sliver broke:
> When down her weedy trophies and she herself
> Fell in the weeping brook. Her clothes spread wide,
> And, mermaid-like, awhile they bore her up;
> Which time she chanted snatches of old tunes
> As one incapable of her own distress.[33]

The pathetic scene has moved all the readers down the ages. A.C. Bradley quotes Coleridge and says:

> The picture of her death, if our eyes grow dim watching it, is still purely beautiful.[34]

This is the last scene of this Act which is the longest Act in the play. It contains seven scenes. In this Act, little by little, death has made its progress. Polonius is already dead, Ophelia dies, Rosencrantz and Guildenstern are on their way to death. Hamlet's death is already ensured. The shadow of tragedy becomes wider and darker.

Act V, sc. i

This is the famous graveyard scene. There are two clownish diggers working at Ophelia's grave and they discuss the manner of her death. No one can decide whether it is an accident or a suicide, and, giving her the benefit of doubt, the coroner has permitted Christian burial. The two of them talk and sing and provide comic relief.

Meanwhile, Hamlet and Horatio enter. After a short dialogue, they start talking with the clown. This man, unaware of their identity, continues digging the grave while talking to them. He throws up skulls of men buried long ago as he digs deeper and deeper. One of these is the skull of Yorick, the royal jester. Hamlet takes up this skull and reflects on mutability.

Then the funeral procession carrying the dead body of Ophelia comes in, followed by the court. Hamlet of course does not know about Ophelia's death, for, it becomes clear, Horatio has not told him anything about it. The two of them withdraw. The priest tells Laertes that though Ophelia's body is permitted to be buried in sanctified ground, no other religious ritual is allowed.

It is then that Hamlet realizes that it is Ophelia who is being buried. Laertes in the excess of his grief leaps into the grave and Hamlet, coming forward, also does the same. The two of them start fighting and the King's men separate them. Hamlet now declares his love for Ophelia and expresses surprise at Laertes's hostility. He does not know that Laertes holds him responsible for the deaths of both his father and his sister. He should, however, have expected it.

Wilson Knight has observed that in the graveyard scene Hamlet "utterly loses his mental control" for the third time in the play. The first time is when he meets Ophelia in the incidents narrated by her to Polonius, the second time in the Nunnery scene (Act III, sc. i) and the third time in this scene.

This scene looks back to the last scene of Act IV in which Ophelia's death is reported, and forward to the next scene because it paves the way for the fencing-match. It is remarkable because it also provides comic relief and the element of spectacle in the burial of Ophelia.

It is written half in prose and half in verse, for the conversation with the first clown is entirely in prose. Before that, the dialogue between the two clowns is also in prose. This is continued till line 205 and then with the entrance of the funeral procession, poetry starts and continues till the end. This part also contains songs sung by the First Clown. It is actually one song, but it contains three stanzas which are sung interspersed with prose dialogue.

The scene falls into two clear-cut divisions: the first part being the conversation with the gravediggers and between them, till line 210. Then the second part, in verse, starts with the entrance of the dead body of Ophelia in procession and continues till the end. It provides considerable variety.

Act V, sc. ii

We come now to the last scene of the play. It opens quietly, with Hamlet and Horatio talking. Hamlet tells Horatio how, on his journey to England, he had got up at night and found the sealed letter entrusted to his two travelling companions. Justifying his suspicions, this letter turned out to be his death-warrant. Hamlet prefaces this account by delivering two of the best-known lines not only of this play but in the whole of Shakespeare:

> There's a divinity that shapes our ends,
> Rough-hew them how we will.[35]

He tells how in that letter Claudius requested the King of England to kill him. He took away the letter (which now gives Horatio to read) and wrote a letter in its place, asking the English King to put the two bearers to death. By great good luck he had his father's signet ring on his finger and with it, he sealed his own letter so that no one can ever suspect it.

This action of Hamlet has been severely criticized, the more so as he does not have any qualms about putting two innocent persons to death. He, in fact, justifies it to Horatio by saying that they deserve it for being so meddlesome:

> Why, man, they did make love to this employment;
> They are not near my conscience; their defeat
> Doth by their own insinuation grow.[36]

The courtier Osric then comes, providing comic relief. He bring the invitation for a fencing-match with Laertes. It is a long conversation in which the dramatist satirizes Elizabethan courtiers in the person of Osric. The fencing-match is to be a friendly exhibition match, not a proper duel. It is repeatedly referred to as "play". The King and the Queen, with the whole court, will be present at it. Osric also tells Hamlet that some betting is going on and the King too has betted on it. Another Lord comes, bringing the message that the King and the Queen are already coming to watch the match. Hamlet is very sure that he will win the match.

The royal couple enters, with all the attendants and Lords and Hamlet and Laertes take their places in a very friendly and courtly manner. The cups of wine are set on a table.

Before they start to fight, Hamlet makes a very gracious speech to Laertes. He says that whatever he had done was the result of madness, and he asks Laertes to forgive him. It is a most moving and gentlemanly speech. Laertes accepts the apology, but is firm in his determination to fight. His speech to the Prince is a hypocritical one, for he does nothing about the poisoned rapier and poisoned wine.

As they fight, Claudius offers the poisoned wine to Hamlet who refuses it. Then, as luck would have it, the Queen, unaware of the nature of this cup of wine, drinks it up. The King observes this, but can do nothing. Here indeed, we have an instance of dramatic irony in the tragic manner. As the match goes on, Laertes wounds Hamlet with his poisoned rapier, then, in the confusion of the fight their rapiers get interchanged, Hamlet taking the fatal one of Laertes. Then, in the course of the fight, he wounds Laertes. Both of them are now poisoned. Hamlet is about to die though he does not know it.

By this time, the poisoned wine has affected the Queen and she dies, warning Hamlet about the wine with her last breath. Laertes, himself facing inevitable death, tells Hamlet that his sword had been poisoned and so both of them are to die. He discloses the fact that the King is to blame and, infuriated, Hamlet at last takes vengeance upon him. Not only does he stab Claudius, but pours the wine down his throat:

Here, thou incestuous, murderous, damned Dane,
Drink off this potion: is thy union here?
Follow my mother.[37]

One by one the characters succumb to death. The Queen is already dead. The King dies too. Now Laertes tells Hamlet that he absolves him of killing him and Polonius and also that he himself is absolved of killing Hamlet. They forgive each other. Laertes dies.

Now Hamlet's last moments have come. His dying speech is one of the most moving passages in Shakespeare. As has been pointed out by Eliot, Shakespeare, like other Elizabethan writers, followed Seneca's theory of stoicism in the last speeches of his tragic heroes. He is dying after having done his duty, but he wants his name to be vindicated:

O good Horatio, what a wounded name,
Things standing thus unknown, shall live behind me!
If thou didst ever hold me in thy heart,
Absent thee from felicity a while,
And in this harsh world draw thy breath in pain,
To tell my story.[38]

The sounds of marching feet and of shots are heard at this point and the news comes that Fortinbras has arrived. Hamlet with his last breath names him as the future king and dies.

Fortinbras enters the stage to find the principal characters dead. He assumes control and orders that Hamlet be given the burial of a soldier. It has been pointed out that Hamlet is the only tragic hero of Shakespeare to be honoured thus.

This, the last scene of the play is also the most eventful. It is written in a mixture of both prose and verse. The entire dialogue with Osric is in prose and it is continued till the entrance of the king. Thus out of 391 lines, about 130 are in prose. After that the rest of the scene, highly dynamic, is in poetry.

The scene is typical of Elizabethan tragedies. All the principal characters die—there are eight deaths in the play and four of them take place in this one. The wrong-doer is punished, and all three revenge actions are satisfactorily concluded. Above all, the disturbed moral order in the kingdom is restored. A noble and efficient king will now be on the throne. All this is summed up by H.S. Wilson when he remarks:

> The catastrophe of *Hamlet* is Christian in its implication. Denmark has been purged of its rottenness, justice has been done and the peace that crowns the end represents the purification of the hero's motive through his submission to the will of heaven, quite as much as the freeing of the state from guilt.[39]

NOTES

1. T.S. Eliot, *The Opening Scene of Hamlet*, in Jump, *op. cit.*, p. 118.
2. Quoted in Verity, *op. cit.*, p. 137.
3. Ellis-Fermor, *op. cit.*, p. 33.
4. G. Wilson Knight, *The Wheel of Fire*, London: Methuen and Co. Ltd., 1977 rpt., p. 33.
5. Act I, sc. ii, ll. 150-51, p. 14.
6. Act I, sc. ii, ll. 254-55, p. 18.
7. Act I, sc. iii, ll. 14-17, p. 19.
8. Act I, sc. iii, ll. 58-77, pp. 20-21.
9. Act I, sc. v, ll. 23-25, p. 27.
10. Theodore Spencer, *Shakespeare and the Nature of Man*, New York: The Macmillan Co., 1945, p. 105.
11. Act I, sc. v, ll. 85-86, p. 29.
12. Act I, sc. v, ll. 189-90, p. 33.
13. Act I, sc. v, ll. 171-72, p. 32.
14. J. Holloway, *Hamlet* in Jump, *op. cit.*, p. 162.
15. Act II, sc. ii, ll. 266-68, p. 47.
16. Verity, *op. cit.*, p. 158.
17. Act II, sc. ii, ll. 582-83, p. 57.
18. Knight, *op. cit.*, p. 25.
19. M.C. Bradbrook, *Themes and Conventions of Elizabethan Tragedy*, C.U.P., Vikas, students' ed., p. 32.
20. Act III, sc. i, ll. 164-65, p. 63.
21. Act III, sc. ii, ll.2-5, p. 64.
22. Act III, sc. ii, ll. 16-18, p. 65.
23. Act III, sc. ii, ll. 352-54, p. 77.
24. Act III, sc. ii, ll. 778-79, p. 77.

25. Act III, sc. ii, ll. 36-38, p. 79.
26. Bradley, *op. cit.*, p. 108.
27. Act III, sc. iii, ll. 96-97, p. 81.
28. Act III, sc. iv, ll. 93-95, p. 84.
29. Knight, *op. cit.*, p. 27-28.
30. Act IV, sc. v, ll. 29-32, p. 98.
31. Act IV, sc. v, ll. 59-60, p. 99.
32. Act IV, sc. v, ll. 158-59, p. 102.
33. Act IV, sc. vii, ll. 173-78, p. 111.
34. Bradley, *op. cit.*, p. 133.
35. Act V, sc. ii, ll. 10-11, p. 123.
36. Act V, sc. ii, ll. 57-59, pp. 124-25.
37. Act V, sc. ii, ll. 313-15, p. 133.
38. Act V, sc. ii, ll. 332-37, p. 134.
39. H.S. Wilson, *On the Design of Shakespearean Tragedy*, University of Toronto Press, 1968 rpt., p. 46.

5

The Major Themes

Any literary work needs unity of theme to give it a good structure. The great Indian work, *Katha-sarit Sagara*, has not been given the status of an epic because it lacks this quality. It might so happen that the construction of a play might meander, and be haphazard and flabby, for the writer may not be a good craftsman, but the message he wants to convey (i.e. the central theme) is so strongly and convincingly expressed that the play gives the impression of being a neatly constructed whole. The theme, thus, is an extremely important part of any work. It is not necessary that a work has only one theme. It might have a major theme, side by side with many sub-themes. Shakespeare's plays are so complex that most of the time there are many themes in one play. Moreover, a complex work can be interpreted, in terms of its theme, from many different points of view and different critics have posited different themes for his plays. *Hamlet* is one of those plays that have been studied from many viewpoints some of which shall now be discussed.

(a) The Theme of Revenge

Revenge, of course, is the principal theme of *Hamlet*. As such, the theme of revenge has been presented in drama from ancient times and it has been compared with two famous revenge plays in Greek drama by H.D.F. Kitto. Later, in Seneca, the theme became extremely well exposed and, since Seneca's plays were all-pervasive in their influence, the theme became extremely popular. In Kyd's *The Spanish Tragedy* the theme of revenge makes its appearance at the very outset of the play, with the allegorical figure of Revenge and the Ghost of Andrea.

In *Hamlet* also it is the Ghost of Hamlet's father who seeks revenge and first makes it clear in the last scene of the first Act. Hamlet says to the Ghost:

> *Ham.*: Speak; I am bound to hear
> *Gh.*: So art thou to revenge, when thou shalt hear.[1]

Thus, the revenge motif is introduced and thereafter it is made amply clear that the chief business of the play will be to see how Hamlet takes vengeance upon Claudius. The different techniques that are used in revenge plays, the ways and means adopted have already been mentioned (*vide* ch. 4., the section on Genre, *supra*). There are, however, certain implications of this theme that should be mentioned.

Revenge presupposes that some wrong, some injustice has been done to somebody which makes the injured person cry out for justice, or for revenge. In other words, the presence of evil is to be uprooted. Evil, however, is a force which is difficult to control and one evil deed leads to others. The man who seeks to avenge the wrong suffered by him thus calls down destruction not only upon the wrong-doer, but upon others as well. Hamlet, for example, kills Polonius directly, is the cause of the death of Rosencrantz and Guildenstern, is the cause of Ophelia's madness and death, is the indirect cause of the Queen's death and that of Laertes, and last of all, kills Claudius directly, avenging his father at last. Yet, these six deaths (excluding that of Claudius and of himself, which bring the total number of deaths in the play up to eight) are not necessary. These are caused, according to Kitto because Shakespeare means to show how evil begets evil:

> Shakespeare's real theme is not the moral or theological or social problem of crime and vengeance, still less its effect on a single mind and soul, but the corrupting power of sin.[2]

This wider implication of the theme of revenge is what made *Hamlet* such a very complex play. Shakespeare, in order to present the rottenness in the state of Denmark, presents many characters who have the seeds of rottenness in them. There is hardly any character who is exempt from this touch of evil (except Horatio). Claudius is already evil, but, in association with him, Rosencrantz and Guildenstern are turned into traitors, Polonius is turned into an interfering spy and Laertes into a murderer.

As Kitto points out:

> Both in *Hamlet* and in the Greek plays crime leads to crime, or disaster to disaster.... But in *Hamlet* it springs in another way too, one which is not Greek: it spreads from soul to soul, as a contagion.[3]

It is this wider as well as deeper treatment of the theme of revenge that has made Shakespeare the greatest Elizabethan writer and *Hamlet* one of the most intriguing of his creations.

The ethic of the revenge-theme is also a highly ambivalent one. On the one hand, revenge is an impious, irreligious act, and on the other, in *Hamlet* at least, it is a sacred filial duty enjoined upon Hamlet by the very Ghost of his father himself. This second view is the most in keeping with the views of an Elizabethan audience. Shaw had put it succinctly enough:

> Hamlet as a prehistoric Dane is morally bound to kill his uncle, politically as the rightful heir to the usurped throne, and filially as "the son of a dear father murdered".[4]

This is the view taken by many modern critics as well. It would definitely have been the view of an Elizabethan audience also. The author of *The Histories of Hamlet* had put it thus:

> If vengeance ever seem to have any show of justice, it is then, when piety and affection constrained us to remember our father is unjustly murdered.[5]

On the other hand, there is the view that the act of revenge goes totally against the Christian ethic:

> Dearly beloved, avenge not yourselves, but rather give place unto wrong: for it is written, Vengeance is mine; I will repay, saith the Lord.[6]

According to this view, the revenge motive is directly against the scriptures and therefore Hamlet should be punished for taking vengeance upon Claudius. This is what actually happens in Elizabethan revenge tragedies. The revenger is successful, but ultimately he, too, dies.

In most revenge tragedies, there is more than one revenge action. In Kyd there are three and the same is the case with our play. The first of the revenge action that we come to know in the play is that concerned, not with Hamlet, but with the Norwegian prince Fortinbras. Horatio clarifies this in Act I, sc. i, namely that this prince wants to avenge the death of his father in the hands of the elder Hamlet. His father had been killed in fair duel, but all the same he wants to avenge it. The second action, which is the concern of the main plot, is introduced in the fifth scene of the same Act when the Ghost enjoins revenge as a sacred filial duty on Hamlet:

> *Gh.*: If thou didst ever thy dear father love
> *Ham.*: O God!
> *Gh.*: Revenge his foul and most unnatural murder.[7]

This revenge action is the main action of the play, but the theme of revenge makes its appearance once more with Laertes. He too wants to avenge his father's and Ophelia's death:

> Let come what comes; only I'll be revenged
> Most thoroughly for my father.[8]

Revenge thus is definitely the main theme of the play. It is present from the beginning to the very end of the play and the two main male characters (Hamlet and Laertes) of the main and the sub-plot are motivated by it. The two other characters of these plots, male as well as female, are the sufferers of this destructive theme.

(b) The Theme of Social Ruin

This is the view expounded by John Holloway. First of all, analysing Hamlet's own role in the play, he says that here we have a certain, well-defined situation. It is a situation that is progressing stage by stage—a situation in which a man is "engaged in a known career". This situation has been deliberately created, Hamlet has been assigned a definite role and he emphasizes it by dedicating himself in the Ghost scene and also by making a ritual of swearing on his sword. Each of the seven soliloquies make it clear that his life is now dedicated to this one overwhelming cause—avenging his father's death.

This situation, this dedication gradually brings about a significant change in his relationship with the other characters. This has been pointed out by many other critics as well. G. Wilson knight treats it as the gradual spread of an evil infection:

> Good cannot come of evil: it is seen that the sickness of his soul only further infects the state—his disintegration spreads out, disintegrating.[9]

Thus, the other characters suffer because of him. Polonius, an interfering busybody, it is true, but with no evil in him, did not deserve to die a rat's death. Rosencrantz and Guildenstern, both well-meaning and harmless creatures are treated as traitors and sent to their death. The Queen, towards whom the Ghost himself shows consideration, is seen as incestuous and lecherous and dies an inglorious and untimely. Ophelia becomes mad and dies. Laertes turns into an ignoble poisoner and dies. Finally, after all these unnecessary deaths Claudius is punished and in the process Hamlet too dies. This is what Holloway calls "progressive" social ruin and further asserts:

> More clearly than almost anything in this work, Shakespeare has made characters speak out of character...in order that their words may guide our eyes and minds as we watch.[10]

He has taken the well-known speeches of Rosencrantz and Guildenstern to emphasize this feature. When in Act III, after the inset play is over, Claudius tells them to prepare to accompany Hamlet to England, they not only agree, but fervently support him, giving voice to some of the inmost beliefs of the Elizabethan about society and statecraft:

> Guild.: Most holy and religious fear it is
> To keep those many bodies safe
> That live and feed upon your majesty.
>
> Rose.: ...The cease of majesty
> Dies not alone; but like a gulf, doth draw
> What's near it with it ....

...Ne'er alone
Did the king sigh, but with a general groan.[11]

According to Holloway, then, these two persons are, in this instance, speaking out of character. The two of them are, to a certain extent, comic and rather despicable figures and one does not expect a dialogue of this dimension and depth from them. The fact that they are speaking with reference to Claudius makes the speeches highly ironical, for it is Claudius who is the wrong-doer in this play, not the guardian of public weal. Shakespeare would seem to highlight this fact by putting such beliefs in the mouths of such characters, on such an occasion, for Claudius, afraid that he has been caught out in his misdeeds, is trying to get rid of his punisher.

(c) The Theme of Over-ruling Providence

H.S. Wilson classifies ten of Shakespeare's tragedies into several groups. Four of them, according to him, expound the "order of faith" and *Romeo and Juliet* and *Hamlet* present the thesis, with *Othello* and *Macbeth* presenting the antithesis. These four are based on Christian theology. *Julius Caesar*, *Coriolanus*, *Troilus and Cressida* and *Timon of Athens* exemplify the "order of nature", for they do not reflect Christian assumptions. *Antony and Cleopatra* and *King Lear* present, respectively, the synthesis of these two kinds of truth. Referring to the first group he says:

> In all four plays of this group a Christian conception of the significance of human action in this world is an ordering principal of the drama.[12]

He then proceeds to analyse the plays accordingly, finding a deeply religious significance in the thoughts and actions of the characters. He finds that everyone in the play and, moreover, every element in it, from the plot to the imagery, points at the fact that there is a sickness in the state which is caused by an overruling Providence. As Marcellus says quite early in the play "something is rotten in the state of Denmark". This rottenness is to be found in the characters and their actions, but this:

> ...is countered by the emergent theme of an over-ruling Providence which shapes the action towards a climax none of the actors foresees.[13]

This is perfectly true. All the characters frequently try to do something and they are foiled at every turn. Polonius tries to spy on Hamlet and has to die an ignominious death, the king tries to get Hamlet killed and fails, Rosencrantz and Guildenstern accompany Hamlet on an embassage and instead are sent to their death. Laertes tries to avenge his father's death and, while successful, cannot save himself. Claudius tries to poison Hamlet and succeeds only in poisoning his wife. Hamlet tries to kill Claudius at his prayers and cannot. It is as though human will and strength is set at naught by some over-seeing Power that has its own design to complete. Only after all the characters who are besmirched with guilt have gone will the sickness in the state be purged. Hamlet is the one character who has a glimpse of this higher reality:

> ...There is a special providence in the fall of a sparrow. If it be now, 'tis not to come; if it be not now to come, it will be now; it be not now, yet it will come: the readiness is all.[14]

Earlier, in the same scene, when explaining how he came to know of the treachery of Claudius, he ascribes the event to the same Providence:

> There's a divinity that shapes our ends,
> Rough-hew them how we will.[15]

This divine Providence has its own plans—something that is not perceived by any one. In spite of everything that the characters might do, it is Providence that leads the play to:

> ...a climax in which justice at length prevails, the land is purged of its sickness, the kingdom of Denmark restored to pristine health.[16]

Very much the same thing is said by John Holloway when he remarks that in *Hamlet* "chance turns into a larger design".[17]

(d) The Theme of Pride

It is the view of G.R. Elliott that all the tragedies of the Renaissance are tragedies of pride. It is not Shakespeare alone who deals with this theme but all Renaissance tragedians do so. Pride reigns everywhere, in different fashions, but still, it is pride. He declares that not only in the tragedies, but in the semi-tragic plays also, our dramatist has treated the same theme from the beginning to the end of his dramatic career. In Brutus, Hamlet and Othello, this trait of pride is not so obvious, but in a subtle manner it is still the ruling passion. He finds a repetition of this theme in plays as different from each other as Hamlet and Coriolanus:

> They have a central theme in common: right self-estimate turning into wrong pride.[18]

In *Hamlet*, thus we see in the protagonist a gradually developing a corroding sense of his superiority over others. It seems that he cannot speak except to mock others. At first it is Claudius whom he mocks but then, gradually, we see that it is not only Claudius at whom his barbed word-play is aimed. But Polonius also comes in for his share of it. Everyone except Horatio, in fact is subjected to his satirical remarks. It is at its most offensive in the scene with his mother. The Ghost had expressly told to take care of her, but he does not respect his wishes:

> *Queen*.: Hamlet, thou hast thy father much offended.
> *Ham*.: Mother, you have my father much offended.
> *Q*.: Come, come, you answer me with an idle tongue
> *H*.: Go, go, you question with a wicked tongue.[19]

This is how he begins, and he goes on in such a way that the Queen is frightened and the Ghost has to interfere. A sense of his own superiority rules Hamlet to such an extent that he treats everyone in such a manner as to make them feel their inferiority. He treats Laertes with more consideration, perhaps it is because he is an excellent swordsman, but except for Horatio and Laertes he is condescending to everyone else, and downright rude to some.

An indication of his self-esteem is to be easily found in the fact that he regards himself as someone selected specially to do the work that no one else can, disregarding the fact that it is because he is the elder Hamlet's son that the duty of blood revenge falls on him, not because of any special trait in his own personality:

> The time is out of joint; O cursed spite
> That ever I was born to set it right.[20]

This idea is expressed repeatedly in the play. In the famous speech on the dignity of man, again, while admiring man as the supreme handiwork of God, he yet finds it in himself to say that man does not afford him any pleasure:

> And yet, to me, what is this quintessence of dust? man delights not me.[21]

This would be possible only if there is an innate sense of the superiority of himself over others. At first, as Elliott points out, this feeling is one of "right self-esteem" but it turns to "wrong pride" and brings tragic doom upon him. After all, the brightest of the angels, Lucifer, fell through pride.

(e) The Theme of Death

G. Wilson Knight thinks that the main theme of *Hamlet* is death. He believes that Hamlet is partially mad and it is because of the actual death of his father and the metaphorical death of his faith in his mother that this partial lunacy has come about:

> Now the theme of *Hamlet* is death. Life that is bound for disintegration, love that does not survive the loved one's life—both, in their insistence on death as the primary fact of nature, are branded on the mind of Hamlet.[22]

The presence of inevitable death and decay, has, according to Wilson Knight, turned Hamlet into a mentally sick person. There is something rotten, not merely in the state of Denmark, but in the mind of its prince as well. Wilson Knight declares:

> Death is truly the theme of this play, for Hamlet's disease is mental and spiritual death.[23]

He dwells upon the various as well as numerous references to death and decay in the speeches, not only of Hamlet, but of the other characters as well. Hamlet's consciousness of death has agonised him to such an extent that he has become nearly mad, and this madness, according to Knight, is "mirrored" in Ophelia's bereavement and her own resulting madness. The Player Queen's death of love for the Player King is reflected in the death of Queen Gertrude's love for her husband. Death, whether real, or metaphorical, is present everywhere in the play. Polonius and Ophelia die quite early in the course of events and the two courtiers, Rosencrantz and Guildenstern, are sent to their death. The Ghost brings in the aura of death right in the beginning and at the end of the play, all the principal characters die. There are no less than eight deaths in the play. Death thus, according to Wilson Knight, is the principal theme of the play. The diligent student should remember that there are many deaths in all Elizabethan tragedies.

(f) Effect of Guilt

In his famous essay on *Hamlet*, T.S. Eliot expounded the idea of "objective correlative" and, while doing so, that Shakespeare is dealing in this play with an intractable idea—that of the effect of Queen Gertrude's guilt upon Hamlet. This is "intractable material" for drama:

> *Hamlet*...is a play dealing with the effect of a mother's guilt upon her son, and that Shakespeare is unable to impose this motif successfully upon the "intractable" material of the old play.[24]

T.S. Eliot is more concerned with the intractability of the old material of the play as well as the new than with the theme, but it is clear that there is no doubt in his mind concerning the central theme. Though the theme may prove to be an awkward one, leading to what he considered to be the failure of *Hamlet* yet it is such a theme that influenced the hero so much that it ultimately led to a tragic outcome. Hamlet considered his mother to be guilty only of too hasty a marriage. This was the situation in the beginning of the play. Then the Ghost calls it an incestuous marriage and this is also added to

Queen Gertrude's guilt. It should be noted that the idea of incest was not there in Hamlet's mind from the beginning. The psychological interpretation given by Ernest Jones interprets the effect of this in the light of Oedipus Complex but even without going to such lengths, it can be said that the theme of the play is the effect of a mother's guilt upon her son, though the injunction of the Ghost should not be forgotten. He tells Hamlet to avenge his death by killing Claudius, but not to let the Queen suffer:

> But, however thou pursuest this act,
> Taint not thy mind, nor let thy soul contrive
> Against thy mother aught: leave her to heaven.[25]

This makes it clear that he does not hold her to blame or that he has forgiven her, which is more than what Hamlet can do, for in the closet scene he is, quite deliberately, cruel to her.

Apart from these, many other themes have been found in *Hamlet*. Theodore Spencer, for example, finds the theme of the conflict between the two natures of man—the optimistic view of man as the crowning glory of nature and the realistic pessimistic view, to be the theme of most importance. In fact, he takes Hamlet's speech on man in which he finds man to be like an angel and yet a quintessence of dust, to be symptomatic of the very nature of this conflicting view of man that is central to the Jacobean Age. The fact that the play is the last one to be written by Shakespeare in the Elizabethan Age lends point to his views. Henri Fluchere, while considering that the main theme of the play is vengeance, finds that vengeance is but a superficial theme. Underlying the theme of revenge is the far deeper theme of man's nature which is made to confront the moral and metaphysical problem of life, the problems of existence. This problem of existence is also a problem of identity. T.R. Henn bases his analysis of the theme on a mediaeval moral tradition according to which evil is generated through sin and should be avoided. But this in turn generates evil in the hero who has an innate nobility that comes into conflict with this evil. Evil thus emerges into action through the personality of the hero and this is the theme of tragedy.

Thus, different critics have found different themes being embodied in the play and often the views of one critic seem to echo another's. All are partially true. The very fact that so many different views about the theme can exist and all seem valid means that they are all based on something that is truly there in the play and supports each view. These should make the earnest student realize the complexity of Shakespeare's plays.

NOTES

1. Act I, sc. v, ll. 6-7, p. 26.
2. H.D.F. Kitto, *op. cit.*, p. 115.
3. *Ibid.*
4. J. Jump, *op. cit.*, pp. 46-47.
5. Quoted in Kenneth Muir, *Shakespeare's Tragic Sequence*, London: Hutchinson Univ. Lib., 1972, p. 59.
6. St. Paul's Epistle to the Romans, 12:19, *The Holy Bible*, New York: American Bible Society, no date, p. 166.
7. Act I, sc. v, ll. 23-25, p. 27.
8. Act IV, sc. v, ll. 118-19, p. 101.
9. G. Wilson Knight, *op. cit.*, p. 20.
10. John Holloway, *Hamlet*, in Jump, *op. cit.*, pp. 166-67.
11. Act III, sc. iii, ll. 8-23, p. 78.
12. H.S. Wilson, *op. cit.*, p. 4.
13. *Ibid.*, p. 33.
14. Act V, sc. ii, ll. 207-10, p. 129.
15. Act V, sc. ii, ll. 10-11, p. 123.
16. Wilson, *op. cit.*, p. 33.
17. John Holloway, *op. cit.*, p. 171.
18. G.R. Elliott, *Flaming Minister*, 1953, pp. xix-xxi.
19. Act III, sc. iv, ll. 9-12, pp. 81-82.
20. Act I, sc. v, ll. 189-90, p. 33.
21. Act II, sc. ii, ll. 299-300, p. 48.
22. G. Wilson Knight, *op. cit.*, p. 31.
23. *Ibid.*, p. 28.
24. T.S. Eliot, *Selected Prose*, Penguin Books in association with Faber and Faber, 1958, p. 106.
25. Act I, sc. v, ll. 84-86, p. 29.

6

The Major Characters

A play is declared to be successful when it has proved to be stage-worthy, and a classic when it has passed the far more difficult test of time. Our poet can be said to stand unrivalled in both these respects. His plays, moreover, have given us a whole gallery of characters who are more than realistic convincing human being for they often have a symbolic dimension, thus becoming universal figures. There are many dramatists who depict their central figures with aplomb but keep their other, minor, characters, vague and shadowy. Marlowe is a playwright of this class. Shakespeare, except in his early plays, depicts each of the characters with so much individualization that they gain a personality that is peculiar to them.

He has also given us more memorable characters than any other dramatist. His tragic heroes, like Hamlet and others, his heroines, like Rosalind and numerous others have become immortal. Other dramatists have given one or two such significant and memorable figures, but Shakespeare has given an entire gallery.

What is the most remarkable feature in his dramatic career is that he never reached a point of stasis in his art of characterization, or, indeed in any other field of his art. As he himself grew older in his life, so grew his understanding of his fellow human beings and consequently, his delineations become fuller and more detailed. Their range and variety increased with each play. The very inmost depths of the human mind were plumbed and all the complexities explored. What Pope had said more than two centuries ago still remains valid:

> His characters are so much Nature herself that 'tis a sort of injury to call them by so distant a name as copies of her.[1]

This is even more the case with *Hamlet*. One of the reasons for the play's popularity today is that modern man identifies himself with Hamlet. This had, actually, started much earlier. Coleridge had, in 1827, declared:

> I have a smack of Hamlet myself, if I may say so.[2]

This sentiment has been echoed by later critics. It must be remembered, however, that such expertise cannot be acquired in a day. It was acquired slowly and paintstakingly. The first phase of his career shows him learning his art and so there are evidences of immaturity. The characters of the second phase already show more understanding of human nature. The important male figures of the chronicle plays are the creations of this time as well as the memorable heroines of the golden comedies. The four heroines of these comedies cast their male counterparts into shade, so captivating and vivacious are they.

The great tragic heroes belong to the third phase. Here a world is presented in which evil predominates. Hamlet, Othello, Lear and Macbeth were created at this time. Such characters are not merely realistic, for they have attained the status of universality and therefore represent the "concrete universal".

In his last Romances, Shakespeare created many more memorable characters, male as well as female. The titanic figure of the tragic hero, however, does not recur any longer. The present work is concerned with such a figure and his associates, though Ophelia, in her innocence and purity foreshadows the later heroines. She however, is a tragic figure which the latter are not.

When creating his characters, Shakespeare had not only real life, but many other supporting elements, to fall back upon. Contemporary customs and stage-conventions were there to provide a base, as also were classical precepts and examples. Rules for characterization had been clearly formulated by Aristotle and practical examples were to be found in classical drama. As has already been pointed out (*vide* Chapter 3, *Life and Works, supra*), Shakespeare had studied Plautus and Terence in comedy and Seneca in tragedy during his school-days. Many other contemporary works on the subject of characterization in drama were also available, like Thomas Newton's *The Touchstone of Complexions*, Bishop Hall's *Characters of Virtues and Vices*, Overbury's *Characters*, etc. These, in addition to rules, also contained sketches of characters. Theophrastus, whose work was translated by Boyes, had given more than a hundred of such character-sketches.

No less a person than Aristotle himself had started the tradition of giving such character-sketches. He had given several detailed characters, running to several pages respectively, in his *Ethics*. Moreover, he had laid down the rules governing dramatic characters in his *Poetics*. All characters, whether tragic or comic, should have four traits: (a) Proportion or Goodness, (b) Appropriateness, (c) Realism, and (d) Consistency. We shall cast a cursory glance at each of them now.

The quality of Proportion or Goodness has two implications. First of all, the moral intention of a character must be good:

> Any speech or action that manifests moral purpose of any kind will be expressive of character: the character will be good if the purpose is good.[3]

Aristotle points out that this goodness differs from person to person as is perfectly plausible. Goodness, he tells us, is to be found in the character of a servant if he refrains from theft, but in a character belonging to a higher class it is natural and expected, it does not carry any moral value.

In the second place, goodness must not exist unadulterated in a character, for that would not be lifelike. Goodness and evil must exist in proper proportion in a character, just as it does in reality.

Appropriateness or Propriety is the second quality. A character should speak or act in accordance with the kind of person he is. Aristotle gives us an example that puts the matter beyond doubt:

> There is a type of manly valour; but valour in a woman, or unscrupulous cleverness, is inappropriate.[4]

There is no violation of this rule in our poet. The characters always speak and act in such a manner as is appropriate to their age and gender and social position. Nor is the rule of Proportion ever violated. As is well-known, in the play under discussion, Claudius is not an unmitigated villain. Shakespeare has made him an able administrator. Besides, he has qualms of conscience also. They make him more human. This rule is observed so scrupulously that when a character adopts a disguise, he speaks and behaves in accordance with the *persona* he adopts. There is no such case in *Hamlet*, but there is the case of the feigned madness of Hamlet and the real madness of Ophelia. When Hamlet pretends he is mad, he speaks and behaves accordingly so that no one doubts that he is mad. When Ophelia becomes mad, there is no doubt in the minds of the spectator or the other characters that she is really and truly mad.

The third quality specified by Aristotle is realism. He points out that this quality is different from the first two but he does not elaborate the point. Shakespeare's characters are always true to life. Their actions and speeches, when the situation is taken into consideration, are always natural and realistic. When, in *King Lear*, Cordelia refuses to flatter her foolish father in the love-test, it is perfectly natural and in keeping with the dignified princess that she is. When in *Hamlet*, Claudius starts up in the middle of *The Murder of Gonzago* and goes hurriedly away, that too is perfectly in keeping with the kind of person he is. Likewise, what can be more true to life than his intrigue with Laertes to kill Hamlet and the matter of the poisoned wine-cup? He has been shown to have killed the elder Hamlet with poison, so it would be natural for him to turn to poison in case Laertes fails to wound Hamlet.

The fourth quality, Consistency, is the most important of all. It implies that the character must remain true to his own nature. Hamlet is presented as a melancholy man, disgusted with the frailties of human nature. He remains so to the end. Subtle changes occur in his character, but they are never such as to make him quite unrecognizable. Aristotle has pointed out that a character can change if such changes can be brought about by the circumstances prevailing in the play and also that the character must remain recognizably the same. Both of these conditions are always fulfilled by Shakespeare.

There were, thus, two main factors which controlled the delineation of characters in drama of the Elizabethan age. On one hand, there were the classical rules and on the other, the practical sketches given by the ancient and the contemporary writers. Shakespeare as well as the other writers of the time had easy access to all these. Yet, it is Shakespeare who has given us so many memorable characters. What is even more admirable is that he accepted the conditions and conventions and, when necessary, also adopted them to suit his own convenience. Henri Fluchere has stressed this aspect of his versatility:

> It is equally undeniable that, allowing for his own peculiar genius, he conforms with the accepted conventions of character-drawing as with other conventions.[5]

In addition to all these features, there is the towering figure of the tragic hero about whom there are many specific rules laid down by Aristotle and his commentators. Apart from these well-known theories, Shakespeare had the practical example of other tragic heroes in Latin and English plays, particularly the works of Seneca, Marlowe and Kyd. The spadework had already been done. The most important rules laid down by Aristotle concerning the tragic hero, in addition to the four mentioned above run thus: the tragic hero must be better than the average, of noble birth and nature and he must have some kind of flaw in his nature. Of these, it is the third feature that is the most important. This has come to be known as "the tragic flaw" which brings inevitable tragic doom upon the hero. Aristotle takes care to point out that it does not involve serious moral flaw:

> A man who is not eminently good and just, yet whose misfortune is brought about not by vice or depravity but by some error or frailty.[6]

This is the famous feature of *hamartia* which essentially means an error of judgement that leads the tragic hero to make a mistake that brings about his tragic downfall. This error of judgement, in Elizabethan times, came to encompass a serious shortcoming in the character, like indecision in Hamlet, jealousy in Othello, ambition in Macbeth, etc. It need not, however, mean any such destructive trait. An imperfection that leads a man to commit a crime, must, of necessity, imperil the nobility of the character, but an error of judgement does not do so. Thus, while Macbeth goes on piling crime upon crime he loses our sympathy and respect, which the ideal tragic hero should not. As Aristotle is careful to point out, the flaw in the character is not a serious one by itself. It is merely an error or a frailty in a man who is otherwise worthy of respect. He clearly says that in tragedy, the hero must be better than the average man and thus inspire respect, thus:

> Tragedy is an imitation of persons who are above the common level.... The poet, in representing men who are irascible or indolent, or have such other defects of character, should present the type and yet ennoble it.[7]

As we shall see, the character of Hamlet is truly that of an idea tragic hero from the Aristotelian point of view. His fall does generate the feelings of pity and terror that are sacred to tragedy.

(a) Hamlet

Hamlet is one of those characters who provide inexhaustible scope for interpretations. Even if the enthusiastic student makes a selection of only a few of the critical opinions on him, he will be bewildered at and overwhelmed by their variety. Let us first consider him as a tragic hero and then we shall consider other views.

He is the ideal tragic hero. To take the most obvious point first, he is noble by birth as well as by nature. Aristotle had said:

> He must be one who is highly renowned and prosperous—a personage like Oedipus, Theyestes or other illustrious men of such families.[8]

Hamlet, the Prince of Denmark, is definitely a "highly renowned and prosperous" personage with a noble heritage. Aristotle also says that we have men who are "above the common level" in tragedy and this too is true of him. He is definitely of a stature above that of the common man. There are critics who have even equated him with Christ. It is Shaw the iconoclast who has done so:

> What happened to Hamlet was what had happened fifteen hundred years before to Jesus. Born into the vindictive morality of Moses he has evolved into the Christian perception of the futility and wickedness of revenge and punishment.[9]

This point of view, with which all may not agree, would not have been possible if he had been below, or even like, the average man. All these however are not so important as the feature of *hamartia*—the flaw in the character which brings about the tragic doom that overtakes not only the hero but other as well.

When we take up this aspect of Hamlet, we see that herein he is the most ideal tragic hero to be a man not exceptionally good, but one with enough human frailty to make mistakes. The tragic hero has to arouse pity and terror:

> ...Pity is aroused by unmerited misfortune, fear by the misfortunes of a man like ourselves.[10]

Now Hamlet, though a prince and nobler than the average man, is yet a man, not a divine or semi-divine being as in many Greek tragedies, nor a subhuman creature. He has the basic requirements for an Aristotle hero—good but not too good; ordinary enough to make a mistake, yet worthy of our respect. The flaw in him that leads him to make an error in judgement, his *hamartia*, is procrastination. Many modern critics, again, eschew this idea. John Holloway, for example, is of the opinion that this generally accepted view is not very tenable. It is Hamlet himself who blames himself for not taking vengeance upon Claudius:

> In the play, apart from the soliloquies, the idea that Hamlet delays can be traced only to two passages.[11]

The first of these is the sparing of Claudius who is at prayers. The second passage is that in which the Ghost, agreeing with him about the delay, says:

> Do not forget: this visitation
> Is but to whet thy almost blunted purpose.[12]

Mostly, however, the delay in the act of revenge is seen as a necessary dramatic strategy which had been spotted and pointed out as early as 1736:

> Had Hamlet gone naturally to work...there would have been an end of our play. The poet therefore was obliged to delay his Hero's Revenge.[13]

But a passing glance at his *hamartia* is not enough to explain the endless speculations about Hamlet's character, for even in this matter, there is difference of opinion. G.R. Elliott, for example, finds the theme of pride as the most dominating theme of Hamlet (*vide* Chapter 6, *supra*). He finds Hamlet to be proud of his superiority over other men. Referring to Hamlet's own attitude to Polonius, Coleridge had pointed out:

> You see, Hamlet, as the man of ideas, despises him.[14]

But Hamlet despises, not only Polonius, but everyone in the play except Horatio and Laertes. This is a general characteristic in him and can be regarded as another flaw in his character.

In the early part of the twentieth century, A.C. Bradley had divided the speculations on Hamlet into three groups: first of all there is the "conscience theory" according to which Hamlet does not avenge his father because he is held back by moral scruples. Bradley does not agree with this:

> When he reflects on the possible consequences of this neglect he never mentions among them a moral scruple.[15]

The second of the groups consists of "the sentimental theory" proposed by Goethe who implies that Hamlet is too pure-hearted and sensitive by nature to commit the bloody deed. Bradley does not agree with this either:

> This man, the Hamlet of the play is a heroic figure. He would have been formidable to Othello or Macbeth.[16]

The third view, which Bradley calls the "Schlegel-Coleridge view" is one that holds that Hamlet is a pure intellectual to whom speculation and contemplation is more natural than action. Partially endorsing this view, Bradley adds to this quality that of idealism as well and comes to the conclusion:

> Hamlet had speculative genius without being a philosopher just as he had imaginative genius without being a poet.[17]

These are the opinions, in the main, about Hamlet's character till the beginning of the twentieth century (Bradley's book was published in 1904). After that there was much more of Hamlet-criticism with different critics holding different views. As has been pointed out above, Shaw compared him with Christ and Ernest Jones gives a psychoanalytical view which holds that the delay and the conflict is the result of Oedipus complex ("he being indentified with Claudius in the situation"). Helen Gardner, after analysing the play, comes to the conclusion:

> Hamlet is the quintessence of European man, who holds that man is ordained to govern the world according to equity and righteousness with an upright heart.[18]

As the century progresses, different views also proliferate. There is the view that he is a man of a detached and nearly inhuman intellect—an intellect that is almost at the point of being destructive through the disenchantment he has undergone:

> Hamlet is not of flesh and blood; he is a spirit of penetrating intelligence and cynicism and misery, without faith in himself or anyone else.[19]

It is this combination of penetrating intelligence and disillusionment that drive him distracted. Wilson Knight believes that, as the play proceeds, Hamlet's mind become more and more distracted and unbalanced. His analysis of men and of the world lead him to the conclusion that evil has permeated the universe. Brother can kill brother, friend can betray friend, wife can betray husband. The physical beauty of Ophelia, her meekness only serve to hide potential madness which becomes actual at the first blow of misfortune. Hypocrisy is rife: "One can smile and smile and still be a villain" and sycophancy is everywhere (Polonius sees what Hamlet tells him to see). All this has driven him mad. For Wilson Knight Hamlet's madness is actual and not an assumed one. Towards the end of the play, he develops a sadistic delight in being cruel—sending his school-friends to their death is an example of this, and so is his cruelty to his mother.

Theodore Spencer, on the other hand, sees him as a man torn by the conflict between appearance and reality. He is fresh from the University of Wittenberg where he has been taught the view that man is the crowning glory of God's creation, the peak of perfection in nature. But what he finds in real life is totally different—treachery, lust, sycophancy are rife everywhere. In spite of being "noble in reason" and "infinite in faculties", man is but a "quintessence of dust". This heaven and earth difference between appearance and reality is the source of his melancholy. Hamlet himself acknowledges the fact that he has become melancholy, though he does not know the reason:

> I have of late—but wherefore I know not—lost all my mirth, foregone all custom of exercises.[20]

Theodore Spencer then analyzes Hamlet's melancholy from the Renaissance point of view. He quotes from a medical work translated from French and published in 1599 in which the melancholy man's description fits Hamlet perfectly:

> the most caitiff and miserablest creature that is in the world, spoiled of all his graces, deprived of judgment, reason and counsel...straying and wandering in solitary places; to be brief, so alter and changed, as that he is no more a man.[21]

Spencer, thus, sees Hamlet as a melancholy man and Wilson Knight as a lunatic. These are but two of the views of mid-twentieth century criticism. Later views by later critics also present a bewildering variety. None of these views, however, is as negative as that of D.H. Lawrence:

> And Hamlet, how boring, how abysmally boring to
> live with,
> So mean and self-conscious, blowing and snoring
> His wonderful speeches.[22]

This is, again, an extreme, just as Shaw's equating of Hamlet with Christ is. The serious student, however, needs to know all points of view.

(b) King Claudius

Claudius is definitely the villain of this piece and as such, is not only one of the major characters but fufills a significant need of a revenge play—he is the wrong-doer who has to be punished. From this point of view, he is the reason for the play's existence. If he had not been there, or been what he is, there would have been no play at all. He therefore merits special attention. It is remarkable, however, that Shakespeare has not painted him as an unmitigated villain. We have a serious analysis of his character by Bradley who finds him "very interesting, both psychologically and dramatically".[23]

He makes his first appearance in the second scene of the first Act. Here, he reveals himself as an able and efficient King. His first task is to get the goodwill of Fortinbras and reconcile him so as to prevent a war. It is noticeable that he does not take any punitive action against him which he could easily have done by sending an army against him and, moreover, which any hot-headed person might have done. Instead, he acts like an experienced and wise diplomat by sending two ambassadors to the King of Norway, the uncle of Fortinbras. Thus he, like a wise man, adopts the proper dignified procedure in any negotiation between countries. As Wilson Knight says:

> His speech to the ambassadors bears the stamp of direct and exact thought and an efficient and confident control of affairs.[24]

He then turns to Laertes, treating him with affection and dignity. When Laertes wants to go back to France, he first of all asks Polonius's opinion, thus paying due homage to the authority of a father in domestic affairs. Then he turns to Hamlet and treats him also with affection and consideration. It is Hamlet who is churlish. He tries to reason with Hamlet, asking him to be a little more circumspect in his sorrow. Wilson Knight points out in this connection:

> His advice to Hamlet about his exaggerated mourning for his father's death is admirable common sense.[25]

He requests Hamlet not to go back to Wittenberg but to stay in Denmark and when Hamlet agrees, he is genuinely happy:

> This gentle and unforced accord of Hamlet
> Sits smiling in my heart.[26]

Up till here, Claudius is shown as a good King and a good step-father. It is after this that his villainy is gradually exposed. In the fifth scene of this same Act, the Ghost tells Hamlet of his treachery. Analysing the character of the villain in Elizabethan tragedy M.C. Bradbrook has pointed out:

> Most of the villains are given some kinds of defect which embitters them and cuts them off from humanity.[27]

Now, it is a revealing fact that this observation cannot be applied to Claudius. Bradbrook has given the instance of many villains who have some grievance against society or some defect or other which has turned them into villains. It is not so with Claudius. Indeed, prior to the Ghost's revelations, Hamlet's reactions to him seem to be quite unjustified. So far as he knows, Claudius's crimes up till now are that he has been elected to the throne and is married to his mother. Out of these the first one, as his soliloquy shows, does not bother him at all. Bradbrook's observation that the villains have a grievance against society that "cuts them off from humanity" can be applied more pertinently to Hamlet than to Claudius tallies more with another observation of M.C. Bradbrook:

> The blackest kind of villain is the lustful tyrant.[28]

Yet even here, if Claudius is intended to be a "lustful tyrant" he is a very mild one. His lust is limited to his lawfully wedded wife and he is no tyrant. On the other hand, he shows himself to be a highly considerate King.

Even after the Ghost's revelations, Shakespeare's portrait of him does not abruptly change into a negative one. On his next appearance (Act II, sc. ii) we see him employing Rosencrantz and Guildenstern to keep Hamlet company and also entertain him. They have to report to him, but there is no cloak-and-dagger secrecy about the business. He does it in front of the Queen, thus making it clear that it is a benevolent espionage, for Hamlet has become mad. Naturally, he needs someone to take care of him and who could be better than his own school-friends? We also learn that Claudius's attempt to negotiate with Norway has been successful, which proves his efficiency as an administrator. Then comes Polonius's surmise that Ophelia's rejection has turned Hamlet mad. He is skeptical but his indulgent treatment of Polonius shows him to be a considerate person. Hamlet shows himself in a bad light in comparison, for his manners to Polonius are churlish.

So far we have seen Claudius's outward behaviour. We come to know of what is going on within him in the revealing aside in Act III, sc. i. A chance remark of Polonius uncovers his conscience:

> How smart a lash that speech doth give to my conscience!
> The harlot's cheek, beautied with plastering art,
> Is not more ugly to the thing that helps it
> Than is my deed to my most painted word,
> O heavy burden.[29]

This points to the fact that though he is not subject to genuine remorse, yet like any ordinary, decent man he is subject to pangs of conscience—he is not a villain through and through, like, for example, Iago in *Othello*. A.C. Bradley has remarked:

> His conscience, though ineffective, is far from being dead.[30]

The trouble with him is, this feeling is not a lasting one. Soon enough, in the same scene in fact, he is plotting to get rid of Hamlet by sending him to England, though no other sinister intention is revealed.

We see him next in the play-scene in which he is taken unawares and quickly leaves the stage, thus giving Hamlet incontrovertible proof of his guilt. His discomfiture, however, does not last long, for he enlists the service of Rosencrantz and Guildenstern and arranges for Hamlet's journey to England.

Then comes the justly famous prayer-scene. His contrition here seems to be genuine enough:

> O, my offence is rank, it smells to heaven;
> It hath the primal eldest curse upon't,
> A brother's murder![31]

Throughout this long soliloquy, his troubled conscience makes him think that there is no forgiveness for him, for he cannot even pray. When he kneels to pray, Hamlet comes and, sparing him, goes away. All unaware of the narrow escape he has had, he confesses honestly:

> My words fly up, my thoughts remain below;
> Words without thoughts, never to heaven go.[32]

In the first scene of Act IV, the murder of Polonius is discovered and Claudius seizes at this chance of sending Hamlet away forthwith. The real motive behind this act is clarified later when he says in a soliloquy how he has written to the King of England, asking him to kill Hamlet. From this point onwards, indeed, no bounds can be set to his villainy. He emerges as a consummate intriguer in the Machiavellian manner. He takes advantage of Laertes's grief and arranges for the fatal duel. As has been pointed out before (*vide* Chapter VI, *supra*) in revenge tragedies it is often the hero's privilege to have the right situation made for him. The villain it is, who, quite unknowingly provides for the hero the opportunity for avenging himself. Thus Claudius arranges for the poisoned wine. It is true that the suggestion of the poisoned sword comes from Laertes and not from him but it has his whole-hearted approval. In other words, he digs his own grave.

Shakespeare has, thus, portrayed him as a man in whom villainy is not an ingrained, inherent quality. He is not, for example, as dark a villain as Antonio of *The Tempest*. There are critics (Wilson Knight for example) who look upon him with sympathy. In fact, contrasting him with Hamlet, Wilson Knight finds that he is more human than Hamlet;

> In the movement of the play, his faults are forced on him, and he is distinguished by creative and wise action, a sense of purpose, benevolence, a faith in

> himself and those around him.... In short, he is very human.[33]

(c) Polonius

It has been pointed out by Kenneth Muir that we see the characters in Hamlet through the hero's own eyes:

> We watch Polonius, or Gertrude, or Claudius, not as they see themselves but as Hamlet sees them.[34]

Hamlet sees Polonius as an officious, interfering fool and that is the accepted view of his character. There have been disputes about other characters—Claudius, for example, has been presented in flattering lights by Wilson Knight, but Polonius is not as important a person as Claudius, so critics have neglected him and Hamlet's view of him has passed almost unchallenged. Yet, as Verity points out, the very fact that an astute statesman like Claudius has given the position of Lord Chamberlain to him is significant:

> His position in the state proves the ability of Polonius: the man whom Claudius deems it worthwhile to conciliate must be a good deal more than "a foolish prattling Knave".[35]

We see him first in the second scene of the first Act, in which he is accompanying the King. Here he speaks only a few lines, requesting the King to let Laertes go back to France. Then in the next scene he is seen with his children. His farewell speech to Laertes is a famous one, as it contains many maxims about how a young man should behave in society. It is a set speech, many lines of which in their terseness and precision, have become proverbial:

> Give thy thoughts no tongue
> Nor any unproportion'd thought his act.
> Be thou familiar but by no means vulgar
> ....
> Give every man thy ear, but few thy voice:
> ... .
> For the apparel often proclaims the man.

... ...

Neither a borrower nor a lender be.[36]

It is indeed a most valuable speech that the poet has given to a sage and old councillor. Such speeches are often to be found in Elizabethan plays. Usually, they are delivered by someone in position of authority (father, uncle) to someone belonging to the younger generation. The elder Knowell, in Ben Jonson's *Every Man in His Humour* delivers a speech very like this to his nephew Stephen. The very fact that Shakespeare gave such a speech to Polonius makes one think that perhaps Shakespeare had not meant to make him such a fool as Hamlet thinks him to be. Coleridge, an astute thinker, observes:

> Polonius is a man of maxims. Whilst he is descanting on matters of past experiences as in that excellent speech to Laertes before he sets out on his travels, he is admirable.[37]

Polonius's careful handling of Ophelia shows him to be a conscientious and affectionate father. He wants to protect Ophelia from disappointment. He knows, being a courtier of old, that princes indulge in flirtations and temporary affairs. Ophelia must not take Hamlet seriously. So he tells Ophelia to repulse Hamlet's advances. The fact that he does so with no ulterior motives is made clear when he talks about it to the King and the Queen.

This happens in Act II, sc. ii. Before that, however, comes a scene for which Polonius has been severely criticized. He is shown sending his servants to spy upon Laertes, in France. In this scene, he is shown in an unattractive light. But it must be remembered that in castigating his role here, modern critics have applied modern rules to his conduct. It would not have been regarded as reprehensible conduct in a father to try to keep abreast of his son's affairs in a time when parental authority had a very important place in the social scheme. A father had to keep an eye over his son—it was his duty to do so.

In Act II, sc. ii Polonius expounds his theory of the reason behind Hamlet's lunacy. He thinks it to be the result of Ophelia's rejection. He has grown old in the court and has seen much, known much. This wealth of experience makes him ascribe Hamlet's madness to this reason and he does not understand that the same theory may not be applicable to all cases:

> "Dotage encroaching upon wisdom" is Johnson's memorable formula for the analysis of Polonius's character.[38]

His theory is received by Claudius and the Queen as a possible explanation of Hamlet's madness and this scene then progresses to a dialogue between Hamlet and Polonius. He thinks Hamlet to be mad yet takes him seriously:

> Though this be madness, yet there is method in't.... How pregnant sometimes his replies are! a happiness that oft madness hits on, which reason and sainty could not so prosperously be delivered of. I will leave him.[39]

He and Claudius eavesdrop upon the Nunnery-scene and after that, he gives a very good piece of advice to Claudius: let the Queen try to get Hamlet to confide in her and if she does not succeed, then let him be sent to England as Claudius wants. This is, indeed, a sound piece of advice, but it is his decision to "be placed, so please you, in the ear/ Of all their confidence" that proves to be his undoing.

Before that can happen, however, comes the play-scene. Towards the end of this scene he comes with the Queen's summons for Hamlet. Here there is a brief dialogue in prose between Hamlet and Polonius which is taken by Hamlet as well as the critics to be a satire upon the sycophancy of courtiers:

> *Ham.*: Do you see yonder cloud that's almost in the shape of a camel?
>
> *Pol.*: By the mass, and 'tis like a camel, indeed.
>
> *Ham.*: Methinks it is like a weasel.
>
> *Pol.*: It is backed like a weasel.
>
> *Ham.*: Or like a whale?
>
> *Pol.*: Very like a whale.[40]

Hamlet treats this with contempt, taking it to be the customary sycophancy of a courtier. Many critics also think so. Again, it must be remembered that Polonius's responses can be interpreted differently—he is humouring a lunatic. This shows wisdom, not sycophancy.

Thus, in the closet scene (Act III, sc. iv), he hides behind the arras. Hamlet comes in and his rough behaviour makes the Queen cry out. This alarms him and he himself cries out. Hamlet mistakes him for Claudius ("I took thee for thy better"), runs him through and kills him. His death is the first in the play. It is an undignified death and H.D.F. Kitto thinks it is justified.

Seen through Hamlet's eyes, Polonius is an interfering fool ("Thou wretched, rash, intruding fool, farewell"), but all the critics do not see him through Hamlet's eyes. Ernest Jones, for example, thinks Hamlet's view to be a "distorted" one:

> It is noteworthy how many producers and actors seem to accept Hamlet's distorted estimate of Polonius, his garrulity being presumed an excuse for overlooking the shrewdness and soundness of his worldly wisdom.[41]

(d) Laertes

Laertes can be considered as a major character because, though he is not present in the majority of the scenes, he does influence the action crucially. He is present in only six of the scenes, but it can be said that he is one of the most functional characters in the play since it is through him that Hamlet meets his death.

Moreover, he stands as a lively contrast to Hamlet. He is a man of action whereas Hamlet is generally taken to be the very prototype of inaction. Laertes goes to Paris which is the city of pleasure and Hamlet comes from Wittenberg which is the city of intellect. Laertes pursues revenge with single-minded directness whereas, Hamlet hesitates and postpones. Laertes has only the unfounded suspicious of Claudius to prod him into direct action for revenge and Hamlet has the Ghost's assurance of the murder. Against these contrasts, there are some points which they both share.

Both of them are young aristocrats though Laertes is not of royal descent. Then again, both of them are brilliant fencers. Much more important than this, both of them have to avenge their father's death. This fact makes Laertes a foil to Hamlet and it is in this that most of the contrast between the two of them lie. Hamlet recognizes this similarity before the duel:

> But I am very sorry, good Horatio,
> That to Laertes I forgot myself;
> For by the image of my cause, I see
> The portraiture of his.[42]

We see Laertes first in the second scene of the first Act, in which he has come to seek the King's permission to go back to France. He does not speak much—a total of only seven lines. Very little of his personality can be made out from this. In the next scene, we see him both as a brother and as a son. He is a loving and solicitous brother to Ophelia. He cautions her against Hamlet, telling her that he is only engaging her in a mild flirtation and that she should not take him seriously:

> Hold it a fashion and a toy in blood;
> A violet in the youth of primy nature;
> Forward, not permanents, sweet, not lasting,
> The perfume and suppliance of a minute
> No more.[43]

He, just like Polonius, does not want her to suffer the disappointment of frustrated love, and so he puts her on her guard.

After this, Polonius comes and delivers his speech. Laertes listens to it all with due deference and then leaves for Paris.

These two appearances reveal very little about his personality except that he is a dutiful son and a loving, caring brother. It is after this, from his next appearance (Act IV, sc. v) onwards, that his character develops. While still in Paris he hears of Polonius's death and comes hotfoot to Elsinore, thirsting for revenge. He, of course, does not know that it is Hamlet who has killed his father and thinks it is Claudius's doing. He gathers together a crowd of supporters and invades the palace. The ease with which he manages to do this is significant when one considers Hamlet's difficulties in avenging himself. Hamlet is there in the same palace with Claudius, he is the people's darling, heir to the throne and has proof positive of Claudius's guilt. Laertes on the other hand, had been outside the country altogether, does not have anything to go upon except rumours and suspicions, yet he rouses the people and invades the palace.

Yet, he is not lost to all reason. As soon as Claudius starts talking to him, he calms down to give Claudius a hearing. Before Claudius can say much, however, Ophelia enters. Seeing her condition Laertes is even more inflamed:

> O Rose of May!
> Dear maid, kind sister, sweet Ophelia!
> O heavens! is't possible a young maid's wits
> Should be as mortal as an old man's life?[44]

Then he is taken aside by Claudius and after an intervening scene, we see that Claudius has told him the truth about Polonius's death. Before his revenge can be planned, however, a messenger enters with Hamlet's letter. Claudius, extremely quickwitted, seizes the chance and proposes a duel. It is here that corruption creeps into Laertes's guileless mind. At first he has no idea what Claudius's plan is, but he yields to the suggestion that his sword will be without a guard, so that he might be able to wound Hamlet. Then it is he himself who suggests that he will poison the tip of his sword:

> I will do't:
> And for that purpose I'll anoint my sword
> ....
> I'll touch my point
> With this contagion, that if I gall him slightly
> It may be death.[45]

Referring to this dialogue, Robert Ornstein says:

> False to himself and to his father's advice, Laertes is corrupted and debased by the hunger for vengeance.[46]

After this, Claudius's idea of a poisoned cup of wine follows and then the Queen comes in with the news of Ophelia's death.

This makes Laertes all the more determined to pursue his revenge.

In the last scene when Hamlet offers him the hand of friendship, Laertes hypocritically accepts it:

> I do receive your offer'd love like love
> And will not wrong it.[47]

This is manifestly untrue, since he has already poisoned the tip of his sword. In his defence it should be said that, just before he wounds Hamlet he says in an aside:

> And yet 'tis almost 'gainst my conscience.[48]

Then he wounds Hamlet, their weapons are exchanged and Hamlet wounds him. He then tells Hamlet all about the poisoned sword and wine. In his last moments, he acts like the noble youth he is, exonerating Hamlet of all blame:

> Exchange forgiveness, with me, noble Hamlet:
> Mine and my father's death come not upon thee,
> Nor thine on me.[49]

In his last moments, thus he regains his nobility of nature. This is a feature common to all Shakespeare's tragic heroes, as has been pointed out by T.S. Eliot. However much the hero might have fallen in our esteem, at the last moment he gains back his nobility. In this play, we see Shakespeare endowing Laertes, who is a secondary character, with this quality which also fulfills the requirement given as the last by Aristotle—consistency.

Laertes, thus, is presented as a character who gains by parallelism and contrast with no less a person than the tragic hero. Noble by nature, he is corrupted by Claudius who has a poisonous influence, bringing out the worst in him. Not only is his death the coveted end of all heroes, that is, death in fighting, but, incidentally he has taken vengeance upon his father's murderer as well.

(e) Queen Gertrude

Queen Gertrude can be considered as a major character on two counts—she is a member of the royal family and she is present in most of the scenes—though she does not influence the action directly. She is depicted as a charming and loveable person since both her husbands love her. Indeed, the Ghost's affection for her is seen to be enduring even after death and that too after she had married his murderer. She is also presented as someone who is not troubled by too fine a concept of morality as her son is:

> It is a wonderful stroke of nature thus to embody for us the fact, which we may easily verify in our own experience, that the most attractive people are sometimes the frailest morally.[50]

We see her first in the second scene of the first Act in which it is the maternal aspect of her personality that gains prominence. She speaks but nine lines in this scene, every time to Hamlet, to plead with him. After this, we learn more about her in Hamlet's soliloquy in which he castigates her for remarrying so soon. Such remarriages were not frowned upon for, often enough, there was political necessity for them. Often, the Queen had to marry the murderer of her husband because he had won a battle. The marriages in royal families most of the time were politically necessary. In this play, also, Claudius was her brother-in-law, had been elected as the King by the populace and she did not know that he had killed her husband. So the marriage is not such a crime as Hamlet thinks it to be. The Ghost's instructions to Hamlet are revealing. It is not merely that he attaches no blame to her for having married Claudius, he also adjures Hamlet not to hurt her in any way:

> Taint not thy mind, nor let thy soul contrive
> Against thy mother aught.[51]

His love for his charming, light-hearted queen has endured even after death.

After this, we see her in Act II, sc. ii in which, alone with Claudius, she too exhorts Rosencrantz and Guildenstern when they come in to look after Hamlet. Thereafter, she agrees with Polonius that Hamlet's madness just might be the result of Ophelia's rejection. In the first scene of the third Act in which Claudius and Polonius decide to eavesdrop upon a meeting between Hamlet and Ophelia, she speaks kindly to the latter, giving her a hint of future favours. Such words, coming from her, are extremely valuable to Ophelia.

In the play-scene, she speaks but three short sentences, though one of them has become a memorable, oft-quoted line: "The lady doth protest too much methinks". This need not have any significant hidden comment on her own character, as it is often thought to have. It may merely be that she does not like the bombastic language and over-acting of the Player Queen. Neither, for that matter, does Hamlet himself.

The longest dialogues she has are in the closet-scene (Act III, sc. iv). Hamlet takes a very high-handed way with her right from the beginning. His behaviour is so rough that she is frightened of her own son and cries out for help. This proves to be the undoing of Polonius for Hamlet kills him. From this point onwards, she is confronting a son who is both mad and a killer. Before she can even collect her wits Hamlet starts haranguing her. He tells her tersely that the elder Hamlet had been murdered and accuses her of having betrayed her godlike first husband in favour of an infinitely unworthy person. She is overcome with shame and remorse:

> O Hamlet, speak no more:
> Thou turn'st mine eyes into my very soul;
> And there I see such black and grained spots
> As will not leave their tinct.
> ... ...
> O speak to me no more,
> These words, like daggers, enter into mine ear,
> No more, sweet Hamlet![52]

But Hamlet's rage knows no limits and the Ghost has to intervene. This, if anything, confirms her belief that he is mad, since she cannot see or hear the Ghost and sees Hamlet talking, as it were to empty air. A little later, Hamlet informs her that he is not really mad "But mad in craft". Her motherly anxieties at rest, she promises not to reveal this to anyone.

Though she keeps this promise, she has to tell Claudius about Polonius's murder. Indeed it is far better for everyone to think that Hamlet has killed Polonius while not in his senses and she realizes this. Even then she tries to soften Claudius by telling him that Hamlet "weeps for what is done".

After this, we see her in the first of the two mad-scenes of Ophelia. As soon as she sees Ophelia, all the warm-hearted gentleness of her nature comes forth. In the same scene when Laertes comes in she is calm in all her queenly majesty and defends Claudius against the accusation of having killed Polonius which is but quite true.

We see her next when she comes to announce the death of Ophelia in Act IV, sc. vii. It is remarkable that it is she whom Shakespeare has chosen to announce the two deaths that occur before the last scene. Her speech describing the manner of Ophelia's death is one of the best set speeches in Shakespeare:

> There is a willow grow aslant a brook,
> That shows his hoar leaves in the glassy stream;
> There with fantastic garlands did she come
> Of crow-flowers, nettles, daisies and long purples.[53]

This lovely speech goes on for twelve lines more and it has been suggested that it is an afterthought. That is, it was inserted after the completion of the play.

The Queen tries to restrain Hamlet when he rages in the graveyard scene and later, like the good mother she has shown herself to be, tries to defend him by saying that he will quieten down later. In the last scene also, we see her offering to wipe Hamlet's face when he perspires.

But now her time is running out. She has drunk the poison and soon enough she falls. But, with her last breath she warns Hamlet:

> No, no the drink, the drink,—O my dear Hamlet;
> The drink, the drink!—I am poison'd.[54]

These are her last words. A.C. Bradley pertinently observes that her last moments are her best:

> Like other faulty characters in Shakespeare's tragedies, she dies a better woman than she has lived.[55]

Indeed, she has shown herself to be the ideal mother in the play. More than half of her speeches all concern Hamlet. Almost the only speeches that she delivers which have nothing to do directly with him are about Ophelia. It is the maternal aspect of her character that has been highlighted in the play.

More than one text of *Hamlet* is available and, in what is known as the First Quarto, the Queen's character is portrayed in a slightly different manner. For example, in this version, she is told that her second husband has murdered her first husband and when Hamlet asks her to help him in the act of revenge she agrees to do so. These points, though significant, do not interfere with the basic picture of the Queen as presented in the text that is being followed.[56]

In a tragedy, attention is usually concentrated upon the hero. But it must not be forgotten that tragic doom overcomes many other character as well. H.D.F. Kitto, conscious of this fact, has not neglected Queen Gertrude. He points out that her end is more pitiable than that of Laertes:

> Gertrude, one of Shakespeare's most tragic characters: she is the first, as Laertes is the last, to be tainted by Claudius; but while he dies in forgiveness and reconciliation, no such gentle influence alleviate her end.[57]

Kitto's analysis of her character is a severe and stern one, for he holds her responsible for the evils that happen in the play. Not all critics, however are so stern. Most of them look upon her as, at worst, a rather light-hearted person. Hamlet himself, in fact, is her worst critic.

(f) Ophelia

Ophelia is the heroine of the play. She is often seen as a contrast to the Queen:

> Her naive piety, her obedient resignation, and her unreflecting simplicity sharply contrast her with the Queen's character.[58]

She seems to be a meek, passive and ineffective character. Bradley has given an entirely viable explanation of this ineffectiveness. *Hamlet* is a play in which the love-interest should not be allowed to gain prominence and therefore Ophelia is made a subordinate character, quiet, passive and unobtrusive:

> ...necessary, accordingly, that she should not be the equal, in spirit power or intelligence, of his famous heroines. If she had been an Imogen, a Cordelia, even a Portia or a Juliet, the story must have taken another shape.[59]

She makes her first appearance in the third scene of the first Act, in the scene in which Laertes bids farewell to his family. She speaks very little in it, but the little she says is significant. When Laertes tells her that Hamlet's interest in her might be just a passing fancy, she is surprised "No more but so"? which proclaims her innocence in these matters. When, after a long speech by Laertes she herself, in turn, cautions him, this speaks of her love for him.

Later in the scene when she tells Polonius of Hamlet's attentions to her, she shows herself to be bewildered: "I do not know my lord, what I should think"[60]

When Polonius, like Laertes, tells her that Hamlet's interest in her may not be at all serious, she protests:

> *Oph.*: My lord, he hath importuned me with love
> In honest fashion.
> *Pol.*: Ay fashion you may call it; go to, go to
> *O.*: And hath given countenance to his speech, my lord,
> With almost all the holy vows of heaven.[61]

When in spite of this, Polonius insists that Hamlet cannot be serious, she gives way to what she naturally takes to be his superior judgement. This is perfectly natural for her, for she does not look at Polonius from Hamlet's point of view but regards him as a wise and loving father.

She next appears two scenes later (Act II, sc. i), to tell Polonius how Hamlet, looking like a mad man, had come into her room. She, like her father, is led to think that her rejection of him has turned Hamlet mad. It is this conviction that perhaps makes her agree to let the king and Polonius eavesdrop upon a meeting between Hamlet and herself. She is ready to do anything for Hamlet.

Then comes the Nunnery-scene. The words she addresses to Hamlet are significant as they imply that her heart has not changed towards him, though she has repulsed him. When Hamlet denies that he had given her anything she gently says:

> My honour'd lord, you know right well you did;
> And with them, words of so sweet breath composed
> As made the thing more rich.[62]

Hamlet tells her "I did love you once", and, in his very next sentence he says "I loved you not". About this M.C. Bradbrook says:

> Here there is not only "the sickening drop from hope to despair", but the fineness of breeding that controls reproach, together with the deeper pain that comes less from personal loss than from a recognition of the degeneration involved for the other.[63]

It is this "deeper pain" that is expressed in her soliloquy that reveals the fact that not only does she sincerely believes him to be mad but also, that she is in love with him:

> O, what a noble mind is here o'erthrown!
> ... ...
> And I, of ladies most deject and wretched,
> That suck'd the honey of his music vows,
> Now see that noble and most sovereign reason,
> Like sweet bells jangled, out of tune and harsh.[64]

After this, we see her in the Play-scene. In this scene, she disregards Hamlet's rudeness and treats him with well-mannered indulgence. This is the last scene in which we see her in possession of all her faculties.

There is some preparation before her entrance in the first mad scene. The Queen refuses to see her. Then the Gentleman's description of her condition, mad and harmless as she is, moves her pity and she agrees to see Ophelia. The mad scenes are scenes of pathos, which again, is a classical requirement for a tragedy. As Bradley has pointed out, out of the three persons she loved, she has lost two, for Polonius is gone forever and Hamlet, she thinks, is mad. Laertes, whose support she needs at the moment, is out of the country. She has no one to turn to in her sorrow and this grief is all the more intense, since she thinks that it is she who is to blame for Hamlet's madness and therefore, the indirect cause of her father's death, who has been killed by no other person than her rejected lover. Bradley, full of sympathy for her plight, has feeling commented:

> ...pathetic as Ophelia's madness is, it is also, we feel, the kindest stroke that now could fall on her.[65]

Ophelia hardly speaks in this scene. Instead, she sings snatches of old ballads which are, if anything, more pathetic than speech could have been. The ballads are such as indicate her grief for her father and her disappointed love for Hamlet:

> He is dead and gone, lady,
> He is dead and gone;
> At his head a grass-green turf,
> At his heels a stone.[66]

Then, after a short dialogue with the king and the Queen she sings about love: "To-morrow is Saint Valentine's day". There is very little of dialogue apart from the songs. The little she speaks is eloquent of the sorrow in her distracted mind:

> We must be patient: but I cannot choose but weep, to think they should lay him i' the cold ground. My brother shall know of it.[67]

After her departure, Laertes comes in, and while he is still there she makes her last appearance. She is carrying wild flowers and she distributes them to those on the stage. Each flower has its own significance. For example, fennel symbolizes flattery and columbine unfaithfulness and she gives these to Claudius. She would have given violet to Horatio which symbolizes fidelity, but fidelity is dead for her:

> I would give you some violets, but they withered all when my father died.[68]

This is the last we see of her and when we hear of her next, it is about her death by drowning.

Ophelia is, indeed, one of the most pathetic characters created by Shakespeare. She is the second person to die in the play. She has been adversely criticized by many critics for her weakness, but, as A.C. Bradley has pointed out, it is this kind of character which is just needed for the play, as the love-interest is not the main interest in it. Had she been a stronger character then that would have hindered the action of the play. Shakespeare could have created a stronger character, but, what is more, he had an innate sense of what is suitable at which place. So he has given us an Ophelia, not a Portia or Cordelia:

> Ophelia, therefore, was made a character who could not help Hamlet, and for whom on the other hand he would not naturally feel a passion so vehement or profound as to interfere with the main motive of the play.[69]

NOTES

1. Quoted by Henri Fluchere, *op. cit.*, p. 131.
2. John Jump, *op. cit.*, p. 31
3. S.H. Butcher, *Aristotle's Theory of Poetry and Fine Art with a Critical Text Translation of The Poetics*, New Delhi: Kalyani Pubs., 1981, p. 53.
4. *Ibid.*, p. 53.
5. Fluchere, *op. cit.*, p.136.
6. Butchere, *op. cit.*, p. 45.
7. *Ibid.*, p. 57.
8. *Ibid.*, pp. 45-47.
9. John Jump, *op. cit.*, p. 47.
10. *Ibid.*, p. 45.
11. Jump, *op. cit.*, p. 163.
12. Act III, sc. iv. ll. 109-10, p. 85.
13. Jump, *op. cit.*, p. 22.
14. *Ibid.*, p. 31.
15. Bradley, *op. cit.*, p. 77.
16. *Ibid.*, p. 81.
17. *Ibid.*, p. 91.
18. Jump, *op. cit.*, p. 148.

19. Wilson Knight, *op. cit.*, p. 38.
20. Act II, sc. ii, ll. 297-98, p. 48.
21. Quoted in T. Spencer, *op. cit.*, pp. 98-99.
22. Quoted in H.S. Wilson, *op. cit.*, p. 47.
23. Bradley, *op. cit.*, p. 136.
24. Knight, *op. cit.*, p. 33.
25. *Ibid.*, p. 34.
26. Act I, sc. ii, ll. 123-24, p. 13.
27. M.C. Bradbrook, *op. cit.*, p. 57.
28. *Ibid.*
29. Act III, sc. I, ll. 50-54, p. 60.
30. Bradley, *op. cit.*, p. 137.
31. Act III, sc. iii, ll. 36-38, p. 79.
32. Act III, sc. iii, ll. 96-97, p. 81.
33. Knight, *op. cit.*, pp. 37-38.
34. Muir, *op. cit.*, p. 68.
35. Verity, *op. cit.*, p. xlvi.
36. Act I, sc. iii, ll. 58-74, pp. 20-21.
37. Jump, *op. cit.*, p. 31.
38. Verity, *op. cit.*, p. xlvii.
39. Act II, sc. ii, ll. 202-08, p. 45.
40. Act II, sc. ii, ll. 358-64, p.77.
41. Ernest Jones, *Hamlet and Oedipus* in Jump, *op. cit.*, p. 59.
42. Act V, sc. ii, ll. 75-78, p. 125.
43. Act I, sc. iii, ll. 6-9, p. 18.
44. Act IV, sc. v, ll. 140-43, p. 102.
45. Act IV, sc. vii, ll. 139-47, p. 110.
46. R. Ornstein, *The Moral Vision of Jacobean Tragedy*, Madison: The University of Wisconsin Press, 1960, p. 237.
47. Act V, sc. ii, ll. 239-40, pp. 130-31.
48. Act V, sc. ii, ll. 284, p. 132.
49. Act V, sc. ii, ll. 316-19, p. 134.
50. H.S. Wilson, *op. cit.*, p. 46.
51. Act I, sc. v, ll. 85-86, p. 29.
52. Act III, sc. iv, ll. 88-95, p. 84.
53. Act IV, sc. iii, ll. 166-69, p. 111.
54. Act V, sc. ii, ll. 297-98, p. 133.

55. Bradley, *op. cit.*, p. 135.
56. Verity, *op. cit.*, p. liv.
57. Kitto, *op. cit.*, p. 109.
58. Ernest Jones, *op. cit.*, p. 54.
59. Bradley, *op. cit.*, p. 129.
60. Act I, sc. iii, l. 103, p. 21.
61. Act I, sc. iii, ll. 109-13, p. 22.
62. Act III, sc. i, ll. 97-99, p. 61.
63. M.C. Bradbrook, *op. cit.*, p.32.
64. Act III, sc. I, ll. 151-58, p. 63.
65. Bradley, *op. cit.*, p. 132.
66. Act IV, sc. v., ll. 29-32, p. 98.
67. Act IV, sc. v., ll. 52-54, p. 98.
68. Act IV, sc. v., ll. 165-66, p. 103.
69. Bradley, *op. cit.*, p. 129.

7

The Minor Characters

There are many dramatists who take care over the delineation of their major characters and do not pay so much attention to the minor ones. Shakespeare, however took pains over the portrayal of his minor characters in addition to the major ones. Even if a character comes on the stage for a very short time, Shakespeare depicts him in a convincing manner, making him an individual. Many of his minor characters, thus, are as carefully presented as the major characters of other dramatists. In this play, Hamlet is such an overwhelming figure that all other characters are cast into the shade. Yet, it has to be affirmed that they are, all of them, sharply individualized. Concerning the order which has been followed in the analyses of all the minor characters of *Hamlet*, it should be made clear here that it is the same order as given in the list of *dramatis personae* in the text. According to this list, it is Horatio who comes first.

(a) Horatio

Horatio, Hamlet's dearest friend, (it may be said, his only friend), acts as a choric character but he is also regarded as a foil to Hamlet:

> He contrasts himself implicitly with Horatio, the man who acts with equanimity to the changes and chances of this mortal life.[1]

The best analysis of Horatio's character is given by Hamlet himself, just before the play-scene. After telling Horatio how much he, Hamlet values him, Hamlet goes on to say:

> Give me that man
> That is not passion's, slave, and I will wear him
> In my heart's core, ay, in my heart of heart,
> As I do thee.[2]

Horatio, in other words, is tranquil in his wisdom and thoroughly dependable. In the first scene of the play, he takes on the function of the Chorus, for it is he who tells us of how the elder Hamlet had killed the elder Fortinbras in a duel which has made the young Fortinbras invade Denmark in quest of revenge. This is after the first appearance of the Ghost. The others are puzzled as to why the Ghost has come and Horatio offers them the explanation, that he has come to warn them of Fortinbras's invasion. When he appears again, he is the only one who is brave enough to speak to him. Four times does he ask the Ghost to speak and gives him good reasons every time. First of all he asks the Ghost to speak if he can do so, secondly, if there is any good action to be done if it will bring him relief, thirdly if he has come to warn them of any danger and fourthly, if it has got some buried treasure. But the cock crows and the Ghost vanishes and dawn comes. Here, in the description of dawn, Shakespeare has given Horatio two of the loveliest lines in the play:

> But look, the morn in russet mantle clad,
> Walks o'er the dew of yon high eastern hill.[3]

Bernardo and Marcellus had called him because they were puzzled about the Ghost and now he proves himself to be worthy of their trust, for he rightly guesses that the Ghost will speak to Hamlet and therefore decides to tell him about it. Thus, he solves the problem of the two officers efficiently and quickly. Efficiency indeed, is characteristic of him.

In the next scene, he meets Hamlet who joyfully greets him and we also come to know that he is Hamlet's fellow-student. He tells Hamlet about the Ghost in a precise and succinct manner. Whatever questions Hamlet asks, and he asks many, are answered quickly and definitely and the result is that Hamlet decides to share their watch that night.

In the Ghost-scene, Horatio cautions Hamlet against going with the Ghost. He is a prudent man and thinks of every possibility. But when, disregarding his words of caution Hamlet accompanies the Ghost, instead of washing his hands of the entire affair, Horatio becomes concerned for his safety. When the time for the swearing comes both he and Marcellus humour Hamlet who makes quite a ceremony out of it and makes them swear not just once, but three times in the manner of a ritual.

He is seen next in the play scene. Hamlet deputes him to watching the reaction of Claudius. Here, it becomes clear that he is the only person to whom Hamlet has revealed the secret of his father's death. It is in this speech that we are given the portrait of him as given by Hamlet. He is the only person whom Hamlet can trust. He says this quite clearly:

> Since my dear soul was mistress of her choice,
> And could of men distinguish, her election
> Hath seal'd thee for herself.[4]

During the performance of the play, he retires into the background but as soon as Claudius has gone, he comes forward and supports Hamlet in his jubilation. He does not speak much in this scene. His function here is to support Hamlet.

He appears briefly in Act IV, sc. v, the scene that contains the two mad-scenes of Ophelia. He advises the Queen to see her, otherwise people may suspect that something is wrong and start spreading rumours. The Queen pays heed to this sage counsel. After this, he does not speak at all but it is significant that when Ophelia distributes flowers to the King, the Queen, Laertes and him, she associates him with fidelity which is symbolized by violets.

His function in the next scene is to merely tersely acquaint us with the fact of Hamlet's ill-fated capture by the pirate vessel, and to faithfully convey the message to the King. In fact, in both of these two scenes his role is a purely though highly functional one. In the grave-digging-cum-burial scene also he plays only the role of encouraging and supporting Hamlet. This he does to perfection and it is exactly what Hamlet needs at this stage.

His role becomes far more positive as the last Act progresses. In the second scene of this Act, we see how Hamlet confides in him the plan Claudius had made for his death and how he had out-manouvered him. He has Horatio's whole-hearted support, for Horatio is shocked at the King's duplicity. Then, when the Lord tells him about the impending duel, he offers to do what he can to postpone it. Hamlet refuses of course, and the duel begins.

During the first part of the duel, he does not say anything, but as soon as the two combatants injure each other and start to bleed, he comes forward. Then as Hamlet, on the point of death, entrusts his future good name to him, such is the depth of his love for Hamlet that he wants to drink the poison that is still left in the cup. But then Hamlet enjoins upon him the task of telling the world the truth about him, justifying his character and his action.

It is to Horatio that the honour of speaking the epitaph of Hamlet is given:

> Now cracks a noble heart: good night, sweet prince;
> And flights of angels sing thee to thy rest.[5]

Just as Hamlet's pronouncements on Horatio reveal the latter's character, so do the comments of Horatio on Hamlet reveal Hamlet's character. Horatio has no doubt and clearly pronounces that flights of angels will sing for his sweet prince, and this though Hamlet has killed Polonius and Claudius directly and Rosencrantz and Guildenstern indirectly. As a matter of fact, the killing of Polonius as well as that of Laertes are in the nature of indirect mishaps. The fact of the matter is, Horatio thinks, in spite of all these killings, that Hamlet is a noble and sweet prince. This is the view that Shakespeare wants the audience to retain. Shakespeare has painted his character in sober colours. He is portrayed as a calm and wise man, available to the hero at all times, even after death.

(b) Voltimand and (c) Cornelius

These two characters have but two appearances on the stage, one in the second scene of the first Act and then again in the second scene of the second Act. In the first of these, they speak but one line in unison, promising to do their work dutifully. They are the two ambassadors whom Claudius sends to Norway. He briefs them about their powers and duties and after speaking this one line they withdraw.

When they come next it is as bearers of good tidings. Their mission has been successful and the King asks Voltimand to explain the whole thing. Then, in a formal, dignified speech Voltimand recounts how they had been received by the old King of Norway who is Fortinbras's uncle and tells of the steps he has taken to curb Fortinbras's invasion of Denmark.

It is noticeable that Cornelius does not speak at all. It is unlike Shakespeare to bring a character on the stage and yet not give him a single line to speak.

These two characters serve to point out Claudius's efficiency as an administrator. He could have sent an army against Fortinbras but instead he sends ambassadors. The two of them serve the purpose of showing how successful his negotiations have been.

(d) Rosencrantz and (e) Guildenstern

These two characters, like the preceding two, go in pairs. Both of them are courtiers. F.S. Boas, comparing them with Salanio and Salarino of *The Merchant of Venice*, says:

> It is a law of their existence for such personages to hunt in pairs. Each seeks to compensate for an entire lack of individuality by an alliance with the other.[6]

Claudius, alarmed by Hamlet's madness, has called them to the court and asks them to find out the cause for it. He and the Queen appeal to their loyalty and their good nature and they respond promptly:

> We both obey,
> And here give up ourselves, in the full bent
> To lay our services freely at your feet
> To be commanded.[7]

They meet Hamlet in the same scene. Hamlet asks them point blank whether Claudius had sent for them to spy upon him. They try to evade, but upon Hamlet's insistence Guildenstern tells him the truth. There is no duplicity in them.

This is the longest scene in the play and the two of them are present almost throughout. The later part of the scene shows the Players coming in and both of them remain on the stage.

In this scene, therefore, they come in twice, once in the beginning to talk to the King and the Queen and then again from the middle of the scene onwards. What is significant is that though they are courtiers, they are incapable of hypocrisy and, because they are truthful, Hamlet regards them as spies. They, on the other hand, think that Hamlet is ill and they have come to help.

We see them again in the next scene when the King asks them whether they have been successful in their mission. They have to report failure. Then Rosencrantz tells them about the play and how Hamlet had shown pleasure at the Players' arrival.

It becomes clear from their talk that they truly believe Hamlet to be mad (so does everyone, including Wilson Knight). They do not think they are spying on him. He is ill and has to be properly attended, and that is their task—this is what they think.

They accompany the King and the Queen in the play scene but hardly speak in it. Then, after the King's hasty withdrawal they reappear with the message that the King is very disturbed and the Queen wants to meet Hamlet. Then Rosencrantz makes an appeal:

> *Rose.*: My lord, you once did love me.
> *Ham.*: And do so still, by these pickers and stealers.
> *Ros.*: Good my lord, what is your cause of distemper? You do, surely, bar the door upon your own liberty, if you deny your griefs to your friends.[8]

This is said in good faith—he really wants to help Hamlet. Then follows the famous passage in which Hamlet asks Guildenstern to play upon a pipe, thereby making it clear that he is not going to confide in them.

The next scene is one of the two of the central scenes of the play and opens with the two of them talking to Claudius. He tells them that they would accompany Hamlet to England. Then Rosencrantz delivers a significant speech, the most serious speech the pair of them have been given. It expresses the Elizabethan view of the function and influence of king in society and has been called "out of character":

> The cease of majesty
> Dies not alone; but, like a gulf, doth draw
> What's near it with it....
> ... ...
> Ne'er alone
> Did the king sigh, but with a general groan.[9]

The King is not merely an individual, but he represents the whole state as well. What affects him affects the entire state. When Claudius is worried about Hamlet it means that Hamlet's madness may affect the entire state (as, indeed, it does, though he is not really mad).

After this, they are seen in Act IV, sc. i in which they do not speak, but are entrusted with the job of finding the body of Polonius. But Hamlet eludes their questions. In the next scene (Act IV, sc. iii) Rosencrantz tells Claudius that they have not been able to get the information and then Guildenstern brings Hamlet in. After Hamlet leaves, Claudius asks them to be with Hamlet and make him board the ship for England. They then leave the stage and this is the last we see of them. We hear about them in Hamlet's speech in Act V, sc. ii. There he tells Horatio how he had replaced the letter Claudius had written to the King of England with one that asks him to put both the messengers to death. He has no regrets about it:

> *Hor.*: So Guildenstern and Rosencrantz go to 't
> *Ham.*: Why, man, they did make love to this employment;
> They are not near my conscience.[10]

This is a serious blemish on Hamlet's character. He could not have been sure that the two of them knew about Claudius's letter, so there was no need to kill them. We can regard Rosencrantz and Guildenstern as having given their lives to the cause of duty. All that they did, they did in good faith.

It says much for Shakespeare's impartial portrayal of characters that the reader can have sympathy for a character whom the hero detests. In tragedy especially, the reader or the audience admires and sympathizes with the hero. Yet, in this play these two characters gain our sympathy as being two good-natured, loyal and duty-conscious men who are unreasonably put to death.

(f) Osric

Osric is a courtier and has been brought on the stage only in the last scene. It is against the custom to introduce a character so late in the play, but Shakespeare has done it time and again. For example, Jaques de Boyes in *As You Like It* is introduced in the last scene.

Osric is an empty-headed person. Hamlet refers to him as a water-fly. As Verity has said:

> Osric is a satire on the Elizabethan courtier. His affected language represents (probably with a touch of caricature such as we get in Dickens) a style in vogue.[11]

Hamlet makes game of him and would hardly allow him to deliver his message. He manages however, to deliver it. A duel has been arranged between Hamlet and Laertes the stage to convey Hamlet's acceptance.

After this, when the King and the Queen enter, Osric is specially mentioned as attendant to the duel, during which he speaks out quite often. Then, after Laertes's death and Hamlet's second dying speech, it is he who brings the news of Fortinbras's arrival. He serves the useful purpose of being at hand during the duel and of giving the news of Fortinbras's arrival at the head of his army.

(g) Marcellus and (h) Bernardo

To Bernardo falls the honour of uttering the first words in the play. He has come to relieve Francisco of his watch at midnight. He and Marcellus have seen the Ghost on two previous nights and, puzzled and frightened, have contacted Horatio to watch with them on the third night. Marcellus enters a few minutes later with Horatio and while they are talking the Ghost comes. After he vanishes, Marcellus asks why he had come at all and Horatio gives them the answer. Marcellus thus serves the purpose of putting the question that would give Horatio the chance to deliver his expository speech. Then when the Ghost comes and vanishes for the second time he says very pertinently:

> We do it wrong, being so majestical
> To offer it the show of violence.[12]

Bernardo points out that the Ghost could not speak because just at that moment the cock crowed and Marcellus supports him in a speech based on Elizabethan superstition about ghosts.

The two of them are next seen in the second part of the second scene when they, along with Horatio, come to inform Hamlet of the Ghost's appearance. After this they are not seen again. Both of them are purely functional characters, serving the purpose of witnessing the Ghost's appearance and telling Hamlet about it. There are many such characters in Shakespeare who make a brief appearance, do their duty and go away never to reappear again. They also provide a background to the play.

(i) The Clowns or Grave-Diggers

These are the two Clowns (also called Grave-diggers) who provide comic contrast and relief in the beginning of Act V. Verity has summed up their function thus:

> The introduction of characters like the Grave-diggers... is intended to give both relief and contrast: the tragic tension is relaxed.[13]

It is noticeable that there are four pairs of characters in this play and the two Clowns make the last pair. The two who make up each pair are hardly to be distinguished from each other. Here, however, there is a little bit of difference, for the first Clown seems to be more knowledgeable than the second. He is also perhaps older than the second for he makes fun of him and orders him about. He sends the second one to get some drink for him. In the meanwhile, Hamlet and Horatio enter and the

First Grave-digger continues digging while singing a song. This is a typical Elizabethan song in its mixing of youth and love with age and death. Then, when Hamlet starts talking to him, he shows himself to be a witty fellow, able to hold up his end in the conversation. He also gives Hamlet the common man's view of the events that have happened at the court, it is noticeable that he answers Hamlet's questions in a manner more witty than informative:

> *Hamlet*: How came he mad?
>
> *First Cl.*: Very strangely, they say.
>
> *Ham.*: How strange?
>
> *First Cl.*: Faith, e'er with losing his wits.
>
> *Ham.*: Upon what ground?
>
> *First Cl.*: Why, here in Denmark.[14]

This is reminiscent of the way in which Hamlet himself had avoided answering Polonius' question and of others earlier in the play. The First Clown then points out the skull of Yorick, the former jester of the King. He does not speak any more.

This scene is in the nature of comic relief. With his wit the First Clown provides the elements of macabre humour in the play. Comparing him with other such figures Una Ellis-Fermor comments that they.

> ...not only come from a comic world, but bring it with them, unsubdued, when they enter tragedy and modify thereby the mood, the conduct, even, it may be, the very nature of the tragic figure.[15]

(j) Fortinbras

Though young Fortinbras is brought in physically on the stage in the very last lap of the last scene in the play, yet he is invisibly present throughout the play. There are continuous references to him from the very first scene onwards. He provides the second revenge action of the play. Though his father had been killed in fair fight by the elder Hamlet he yet seeks revenge, and to that end invades Denmark.

Fortinbras serves as a foil to Hamlet because the latter compares himself with him when he meets the captain of his army just before embarking for England. Hamlet reproaches himself for his inaction, contrasts himself with Fortinbras's energetic measures to avenge himself. Hamlet describes him as a delicate and tender prince and chooses him as his successor:

> But I do prophesy the election lights
> On Fortinbras: he has my dying voice.[16]

Then Fortinbras comes in. He symbolizes the power that restores the moral order in the world that tragedy has disrupted. He, with quiet assurance takes up the reins of administration:

> And call the noblest to the audience.
> For me, with sorrow I embrace my fortune:
> I have some rights of memory in this kingdom,
> Which now to claim my vantage doth invite me.[17]

He is the last character to be introduced in the play and he comes in only to end it in a fitting manner. He is the most successful of the three avengers:

> Fortinbras is thus able to avenge his father's death, not merely regaining the territory he forfeited, but acquiring the whole country of Denmark.[18]

(k) The Ghost

The Ghost is a class by himself. Shakespeare does not list him among the *Dramatis Personae*. His name is given right at the end, separately. Yet the Ghost is one of the most important characters in the play though he appears only three times. He occupies a crucial position in the play as it is the information he gives which is the cause for the entire play. *Hamlet* would not have existed if the Ghost had not been there.

Shakespeare had two venerable authorities for brining the Ghost in. First of all, it is there in the sources he had used and secondly Aristotle approves of the supernatural element in plays. Besides these, it was a convention for revenge plays to have Ghosts in them. In Kyd's *The Spanish Tragedy* it is the supernatural figures of Andrea's Ghost and the allegorical figures of Revenge who begin the play. Shakespeare has made use of the supernatural element in many ways in his plays, like fairies in *A Midsummer Night's Dream* and the witches and apparitions in *Macbeth*. In this play, the Ghost does not merely provide thrills and sensational spectacle, it is a dramatic necessity.

There had been some doubts in the minds of critics (as indeed in the minds of Hamlet and Horatio as well) as to whether the Ghost is really the Ghost of the elder Hamlet or whether he is a devil. Hamlet himself says:

> The spirit that I have seen
> May be the devil: and the devil hath power
> To assume a pleasant shape.[19]

Then again, the view that he is a devil is supported by the fact the Queen cannot see or hear him in the closet-scene. These and some other reasons have made some critics think that the Ghost is actually a devil. Now however these doubts have been laid to rest and the authenticity of the Ghost has come to be generally accepted. There are two reasons why the Queen cannot see him. First of all, according to Elizabethan beliefs, a ghost could choose to make himself visible or audible to even one person in a group. The second explanation is more appealing to modern sensibilities. It has been suggested that the Queen cannot see or hear him because she is not worthy of it:

> Does it not suggest that it is her perfidy that seals her eyes? that the coarsening of her nature has dulled her sense of things non-material and sundered her far indeed from the spiritual world?[20]

In any case, the Ghost supplies the motive for revenge. It is he who is the reason for the existence of this play. He comes again and again to the upper world and on his fifth appearance, finally establishes contact with Hamlet. It must not be forgotten that Bernardo and Marcellus had seen him twice before the play begins, so his first appearance in the play is actually his third. Then he takes Hamlet apart and reveals the secret of his murder, enjoining revenge upon him as a sacred duty:

> *Ham.*: speak; I am bound to hear.
> *Ghost*: so art thou to revenge, when thou shalt hear.
> ... ...
> If thou didst ever thy dear father love,—

Ham.: O God!

G.: Revenge his foul and most unnatural murder.[21]

Along with this duty, the Ghost also tells him that he must not harm Gertrude. Ever after his gruesome death and her second marriage to, of all persons, his murderer, he says this, making one think that he still loves her.

This surmise is strengthened on his next appearance in the closet-scene, Act III, sc. iv. In this scene Hamlet behaves to Gertrude with such roughness that she becomes afraid of her own son which makes her cry out. This in turn makes Polonius, hiding behind the curtains, also cry out and then Hamlet kills him so the Queen is now talking to a murderer and, she believes, a dangerous lunatic. Hamlet goes on chiding her till she can bear it no more and asks him to stop saying any more to her. She has to say this three times and still Hamlet does not desist. Then the Ghost appears. He appears only to Hamlet, perhaps in order to spare the Queen who is already frightened. He says:

But look, amazement on thy mother sits:
O, step between her and her fighting soul.[22]

He does not speak any more but vanishes. He had come, at least so he tells Hamlet, to prod him into action:

...this visitation
Is but to whet thy almost blunted purpose.[23]

That is understandable. But he appears just at the moment when Hamlet's harassing of his mother has become unbearable to her and interrupts him. This argues a care for his charming but faithless wife which has endured even after his own death.

Verity has neatly summed up the effects of the Ghost's appearance under, three heads: (a) plot, (b) character-interest, and (c) atmosphere. As far as the first of these goes it has been already mentioned that he is vital to the plot. If he had not revealed the secret of his death there would have been no play at all, for he is the only one who can do so. The characters are all influenced by his appearance, and the third is self-evident for his appearance gives a different dimension to it.

Besides these, there are some more minor characters in the play, such as the Gentlemen who tells the Queen about Ophelia, the priest who attends her burial, and the Lord who comes to tell Hamlet about the duel. These play such very minor parts that they have not been considered separately. As it is, Bradley has observed:

> All the persons in *Hamlet* except the hero are minor characters, who fail to rise to the tragic level.[24]

NOTES

1. K. Muir, *op. cit.*, p. 66.
2. Act III, sc. ii, ll. 69-72, p. 67.
3. Act I, sc. i, ll. 166-67, p. 9.
4. Act II, sc. ii, ll. 61-63, p. 66.
5. Act V, sc. ii, ll. 347-48, p. 135.
6. Verity, *op. cit.*, p. 157.
7. Act II, sc. ii, ll. 29-32, p. 39.
8. Act III, sc. ii, ll. 318-22, pp. 75-76.
9. Act III, sc. iii, ll. 15-23, p. 78.
10. Act V, sc. ii, ll. 55-57, p. 124.
11. Verity, *op. cit.*, p. 207.
12. Act I, sc. i, ll. 143-44, p. 8.
13. Verity, *op. cit.*, p. 114.
14. Act V, sc. i, ll. 150-55, pp. 117-18.
15. Eills-Fermor, ll., *op. cit.*, p. 139.
16. Act V, sc. ii, ll. 342-3, p. 135.
17. Act V, sc. ii, ll. 375-78, p. 136.
18. Kenneth Muir, *op. cit.*, p. 63.
19. Act II, sc. ii, ll. 576-78, p. 57.
20. Verity, *op. cit.*, p. xxii.
21. Act I, sc. v, ll. 6-25, pp. 26-27.
22. Act III, sc. iv, ll. 111-12, p. 85.
23. Act III, sc. iv, ll. 109-110, p. 85.
24. Bradley, *op. cit.*, p. 128.

8

The Plot-Structure

Aristotle has listed the plot as the first of the six elements of tragedy. It is the most important of them and he calls it "the soul of tragedy". He had laid down many rules about the plot of a tragedy and the Elizabethans knew them quite well. We shall now have a glance at some of the basic ideas given by Aristotle.

(a) The Classical Rules

Let us, first of all, keep in mind Aristotle's famous definition of tragedy:

> Tragedy, then is the imitation of an action that is serious, complete, and of a given magnitude; in language embellished with each kind of artistic ornament, the several kinds being found in separate parts of the play; in the form of action, not of narrative; through pity and fear affecting the proper purgation of these emotions.[1]

This definition has many complexities which have been expounded by later commentators. There is no need for us to go into them. The earnest student, like the Elizabethans, should treat this as a point of reference for the rules that follow. The features of tragedy that shall be mentioned all hark back to it.

The most obvious and well-known among the rules concerning plot are the rules of the Unities: (a) the Unity of Action, (b) the Unity of Time, and (c) the Unity of Place. Shakespeare did not take these rules very seriously and but barely followed them.

(a) *The Unity of Action:* This is the most important of the three Unities and refers directly to the definition given above. In this definition, Aristotle has said that the action of a tragedy is "serious" and this rule implies that there should not be any mingling of serious and comic actions in a tragedy. This rule is specially relevant for tragedies, for pity and terror which are the emotions roused by serious action, are the emotions relegated to tragedy. Shakespeare does not observe this rule in the play under discussion or in other tragedies. Hamlet's word-play with Polonius frequently arouse laughter as indeed, the Grave-diggers also do.

(b) *The Unity of Time:* The time covered by the play should be just as much as is covered by the actual performance on the stage. This, actually, is almost an impossible ideal. Aristotle therefore, allows "a single revolution of the sun", that is, the story of a play should take about a full day. This is difficult, but not impossible. Ben Jonson, for example, takes only one day for his plays.

Our poet does not care much for the rules. In the chronicle plays, it is not possible to observe a rule like this. As far as *Hamlet* is concerned, it cannot be said with certainty how much time the play covers. From references in the play itself it can be surmised to be about four months:

> The events of *Hamlet* may be supposed to take place in about eight days distributed at about four months.[2]

(c) *The Unity of Place:* This rule dictates that all the action of the play should take place in one place only. It should, however, be borne in mind that Aristotle did not specifically refer to it. The idea came to the Elizabethans from the writers of the Italian Renaissance: Scaliger, Minturno, Castelvestro *et al.* who had misread Aristotle. Anyway, the unity of place, as it was understood, was very difficult to follow and the only

Elizabethan dramatist who observes it is Ben Jonson, though even in his plays all the scenes do not follow it in Hamlet. There are frequent changes of scenes (*Vide* ch. 5, *supra*).

The neo-classical critics of his own time and of later times had condemned Shakespeare for not observing these rules. All criticisms in this respect have been answered once and for all by Dr. Johnson. His defence of Shakespeare in this respect has become famous.

Many other rules regarding the plot of tragedy had been laid down by Aristotle, and expounded by later scholars. One of them was Donatus who had explained Aristotle's theories in detail and had also expanded them. According to him, the first section of a play is the Prologue. This is usually a speech occurring before the actual action starts. Marlowe's Prologue to Dr. Faustus is a very good example of a Prologue in the classical manner. Shakespeare, too, has written prologues within the first scene of the play, as is the case with *Hamlet*. The dialogue between Francisco and Bernardo is in the nature of a prologue.

There are certain other classical rules to be observed in a tragedy. *Peripeteia* or Reversal is one of them. It implies the fall of the hero from a high to a low status. According to Aristotle, the ideal plot for tragedy is that which involves the fall of a rather good man from prosperity to adversity. We see this in *Hamlet* for in it, a mighty and intellectually great prince is brought to a state in which he is believed to be mad by everyone, kills an inoffensive person and dies in a duel.

Anagnorisis or Recognition is another very important part of the tragic plot. This, at its most superficial level, involves the mutual recognition of two characters who had been separated, as happens in *Twelfth Night*. When Viola and Sebastian recognize each other it is *anagnorisis* of this kind. The most subtle recognition is that which occurs when a character recognizes his own nature. *Anagnorisis* of different kinds occurs in *Hamlet*. When the Ghost comes in for the first time, both Bernardo and Marcellus recognize him, and so does Horatio:

Bernardo: Looks it not like the king? mark it, Horatio.

Hor.: Most like it: it harrows me with fear and wonder.[3]

Then when Hamlet sees the Ghost, he too recognizes him. The most subtle kinds of recognition however, are to be seen in his soliloquies, the most emphatic of them occurs just after the Players have left:

O, what a rogue and peasant slave am I!
Is it not monstrous, that this player here,
But in a fiction, in a dream of passion,
Could force his soul ... ...
... ...
Yet I,
A dull and muddy rascal, peak,
Like John a dreams, unpregnant of my cause,
And can say nothing.[4]

Another important part of the plot, listed by Aristotle after *Peripeteia* and *Anagnorisis*, is *Pathos* or the scene of Suffering. This comprises death, physical pain, etc. The deaths of the Queen, Laertes and Hamlet of course belong to this category but Shakespeare has given such scenes, a new dimension by bringing in the two mad-scene of Ophelia (*vide* her character in ch. 8).

(b) Certain Elizabethan Features

According to classical rules, it is taken for granted that a tragedy should have but one plot.

There might be intrigues, but a sub-plot goes against the rule. Sub-plots are permitted in comedies, particularly in the New Comedies, but not in tragedies. It was the Elizabethan dramatist who used more than one plot in a tragedy. Added to this, the sub-plot is usually a comic one and this violates the unity of action. This however, is not the case with *Hamlet* because in it the sub-plot concerning Polonius and his family repeats the theme of the main plot.

It is one of the remarkable features of an Elizabethan play that the different plots are not just arbitrarily tumbled together. There is a definite relationship between the main plot and the sub-plot, even if there are several of them instead of just one. This relationship can be of many kinds and has been studied painstakingly. It is difficult to find a play that has only one plot. All the plays of Ben Jonson, for example, are multiple-plotted or at least double-plotted. In Shakespeare's play, also, indeed, in the other plays of this time, this is a common feature. He gives two or more plots and neatly welds them together. As shall be seen in a later section of this chapter, this is the case with *Hamlet* too.

The supernatural element is one of the well-known features of Elizabethan plays. It is present in our play from the very beginning. The presence of such elements, the element of "the marvellous" was recognized and appreciated by Aristotle:

> The marvellous should be represented in tragedy... The marvellous is a source of pleasure.[5]

Aristotle regards the marvellous as a pleasure-giving phenomenon, because in Greek tragedies it really is so. It was the Elizabethan dramatists who used the marvellous (the most familiar example being *Macbeth*) to inspire fear and awe. Aristotle has another remark:

> Probable impossibilities are to be preferred to improbable possibilities.[6]

Later critics and dramatists, following these two guidelines have developed their own theories of the supernatural. Ghosts, fairies and other supernatural entities formed part of Elizabethan beliefs, together with many superstitions concerning them. There were several treatises containing information about them, notably Reginald Scot's *Discovery of Witchcraft* (1584), Burton's *Anatomy of Melancholy* and Lewes Lavater's *Of Ghosts and Spirites Walking by Nyght*. These and many other books were available to Shakespeare and to other dramatists and reader of the time.

The Ghost in *Hamlet* plays an extremely important part because it plants the seed of the ensuring action. So in a sense, though it is not a human character it permeates the play. It has, in all, five appearances in the play, twice in Act I, sc. i, once in

Act I, sc. iv, once in Act I, sc. v, and once in the closing scene of Act III. C.S. Lewis, however, counts his appearances as three.

The Ghost is an usual feature of revenge tragedies (*vide* Ch. VI, *supra*). As has already been pointed out, the Ghost of Andrea in Kyd's *The Spanish Tragedy* who can be taken as the prototype of the ghosts in such plays, is present on the stage from the very first scene. There has been doubt in the authenticity of the Ghost (*vide* Ch. VIII, *supra* for the Ghost's character) but ultimately there is no doubt about him in Hamlet's mind. There is difference of opinion among the critics. Eleanor Prosser, for example, thinks that the Ghost is not a penitent soul from purgatory, but a devil. This view is not shared by all. The German critics Gervinus denies any existence to the Ghost. To him, it is a creation of the imagination of the beholder:

> That they see Ghost is, with both Hamlet and Marcellus, the strongest proof of the powers of the imaginative faculty.... Shakespeare's spirit-world signifies nothing but the physical embodiment of the image conjured up by a lively fancy.[7]

H.S. Wilson, after analyzing different views, reaches certain conclusions. First of all he says that Shakespeare has left the status of the Ghost ambiguous. All the same, three issues are clear: (1) that the Ghost functions in a context of Christian significance, (2) that the Ghost enjoins upon his son a duty that a professing Christian must regard as a grave sin, and (3) Hamlet accepts the obligation imposed by the Ghost without trying to understand what warrant he has for so doing.[8]

This third feature undergoes a change later, for Hamlet starts having doubts about the Ghost and arranges for the play.

The Ghost, as has been pointed out by Verity, influences the play in three ways: it influences the character, the plot and the atmosphere.

Its influence on the plot is of the gravest importance. It is because of the Ghost that the play, with its revenge motif, at all comes into existence. Hamlet loathes his uncle, but he would not have done anything until instigated by the Ghost. Even after being told by the Ghost to "Revenge his foul and most unnatural murder", he delays and hesitates so that the Ghost has to reprimand him in the closet-scene. His appearance in the closet-scene is most significant for he tells Hamlet to pursue his aim of revenge, thus once more influencing the plot.

The other influences of the Ghost on the play concern the characters and the atmosphere, which is outside the scope of this chapter. They have already been discussed elsewhere (*vide* Ch. V and Ch. VIII). Much has been said about the Ghost. Let us, for the present, bear in mind that the appearance of the Ghost is fully in accordance with Elizabethan customs.

Soliloquies are an important feature of Elizabethan plays and they are so important in *Hamlet* that they need separate consideration. Soliloquies are speeches delivered by a character when he is alone on the stage. They deal with the speaker's thoughts. They are like talking aloud. In *Hamlet* there are seven soliloquies by Hamlet and one by Claudius.

Each of Hamlet's soliloquies is self-revealing. They make the reader familiar with most of his thoughts and feelings. As H.S. Wilson points out:

> The soliloquies are masterly studies of Hamlet's self-absorption, of the half-conscious dramatization of himself by a young man entangled in a serious dilemma.[9]

In the first soliloquy ("O that this too too solid flesh would melt" Act I, sc ii), Hamlet expresses his disgust with the world as a corrupt place. He has found the lack of loyalty in his mother who has remarried barely two months after the death of her first husband. By analogy, he stretches this lack of loyalty to the entire world. As yet, he does not know that she has married, though unknowingly, the murderer of her husband, yet he is so bitter that he hates Claudius. He expands this idea to include all women: "Frailty thy name is woman." This tendency of Hamlet to rise to generalization from particular instances had been pointed out by Coleridge.

The soliloquy that follows the revelations made by the Ghost ("O all you host of heaven" Act I, sc. v) is not considered to be one of his great soliloquies. Yet, it is a most dramatic one, portraying the extreme agitation of his mind. He accepts the sacred task laid upon him without hesitation:

> And thy commandment all alone shall love
> Within the book and volume of my brain.[10]

Here there is no hesitation in him—they all come later. He will start to think that the Ghost may not be his father's Ghost at all, but a devil.

The next soliloquy ("O what a rogue and peasant slave am I" Act II, sc. ii) occurs just after he has talked to the players. He indulges in violent self-deprecation as he realizes the difference between real action and stage-performance. It is a pretty long speech and Shakespeare describes graphically the thoughts and emotions that are running through his mind. The soliloquy, however, does not end inconclusively, for in it he tells us about the play:

> The play's the thing
> Wherein I'll catch the conscience of the king.[11]

The next soliloquy "To be or not to be" (Act III, sc. i) is the best-known of them. It is generally believed that Hamlet is debating over the ethical complexities of committing suicide, but Kenneth Muir does not think so. According to him, Hamlet is thinking of his own death not directly, but in a roundabout manner:

> In the opening lines of the soliloquy, Hamlet is not discussing whether to kill himself or not.... He certainly thinks that the killing of the king may involve his own death. He therefore proceeds without a break to consider the felicity of dying.[12]

This soliloquy is thought to have shown psychological growth in Hamlet. Even after the Ghost's revelations, Hamlet has gone on growing emotionally, intellectually and spiritually. This soliloquy shows this growth.

The next soliloquy "'Tis now the very witching time of night" (Act III, sc. ii) is a short one in which Hamlet steels himself to talk roughly to his mother. He loves her, but he would be severe with her:

> I will speak daggers to her, but use none
> My tongue and soul in this be hypocrites.[13]

He is cautioning himself against using violence with her, but actually he behaves so roughly that he frightens her. In this soliloquy, Hamlet is in a blood-thirsty mood, ready to kill Claudius.

Yet when the actual opportunity comes he does not take it. As the next soliloquy shows ("Now might I do it pat", Act III, sc. iii) he spares Claudius because he is praying, though his motives are no noble ones.

The next one "How all occasions" (Act IV, sc. iv) is again another self-derogatory soliloquy like the third ("O what a rogue, Act II, sc. ii). As Bradley has pointed out, though this soliloquy is dramatically not important, yet it reveals his character. He is puzzled at himself because he cannot understand why he is delaying his revenge. As Kenneth Muir points out:

> It is a curious paradox that the one intellectual among Shakespeare's tragic heroes should be least able to know why he acts or fails to act.[14]

All these soliloquies have been analyzed in great detail and have been interpreted in various ways. They form part of the intriguing complexity of Hamlet's character and in the process, enhance the complexity of the play itself. In no other play are the soliloquies so important as in *Hamlet*.

The play-within-the-play is another well-known feature that the Elizabethans used for introducing different levels of acting, M.C. Bradbook observes:

> The play-within-the-play was the most useful of all these modifications of the acting. It allows for shadow-work and ironic interplay.[15]

The inset play serves many purposes in such tragedies. First of all, it is one of the ways in which the wrong-doer digs his own grave, as has been observed by Helen Gardner. It has been pointed out in particular about *Hamlet* by Verity:

> Claudius lays the trap for himself. He probably has known Hamlet's particality for the drama.[16]

Such plays, moreover, often echo and parallel the main action of the play itself. Thus the second playlet in *The Spanish Tragedy* echoes the main action and *The Murder of Gonozago* also parallels the main action in *Hamlet*. It is this feature that produces the "ironic interplay" mentioned by Bradbrook. Thus in it the ironic implications are so strong that Claudius cannot stand it and betrays his guilt to Hamlet.

The play is preceded by a dumb-show. This is a feature inherited from the Moralities and usually it reflects the play it precedes. The entire action of the play is forecast and it is surprising that Claudius does not react to it. As Verity suggests, probably the King and the Queen had not paid any attention to it.

The language of the play-within-the play is most often quite stilted and rhetorical, after the manner of Senecan tragedies. Kyd's two playlets and the one in Hamlet are all written in this kind of style. Hamlet had said that he would insert a speech in the play. It is not clear which lines these are. There is no difference in style to serve as a pointer. The playlet and the Dumb-show supply the element of spectacle.

(c) The Sources of *Hamlet*

It was almost a custom for the Elizabethan dramatists to take the material for their plays from many different works already in existence. Translations of classical histories and other works, old plays, narrative poems, romances and such other documents were used to provide the story of their plays. As far as Shakespeare is concerned, the study of his source materials has become an important aspect of scholarly studies. It is highly instructive as well as illuminating to see how he selected the material from six or seven different sources, rejected some, retained some, elaborated some and modified some in accordance with his needs. Verity has summed it up in his succinct manner thus:

> His position was that of the Greek tragedians. He dealt with existing material of drama.... Much as they dealt with the cycles of Greek national a myth; and

> exercising the same sovereign liberty of appropriation, he turned it to the same inspired account.[17]

As far as *Hamlet* is concerned, there are many possible sources:

(1) *Historia Danica* by Saxo Grammaticus, written in Latin and extending through sixteen volumes, dealing with the history and legends as well as the customs and legal code, of the Danish people up to 1186.

(2) *Histoires Tragiques* 1570 by Belleforest.

(3) *Ur-Hamlet* by Kyd.

(4) *The Histoire of Hamlet*—translated from French.

The story was a well-known one in Danish history. Hamlet's father's name was Horwendil and his brother's name was Fengo (which Shakespeare has turned to Claudius). The Queen's name was Gerutha (Gertrude in Shakespeare). The story is the same up till Hamlet's journey to England, but after that it is changed by our dramatist. In the original version, Hamlet arrives in England, marries the King's daughter and then after some time returns to Denmark when he finally takes vengeance upon his uncle and becomes King in his place. Then he comes to England again, marries two wives one of whom finally betrays him. As can be seen, Shakespeare has considerably altered the later part of the story.

Polonius's murder is given in the story as it is in the play. Ophelia and Hamlet also exist in the original story as it has been given by Shakespeare, for Amleth pretends to be mad and a beautiful girl is sent to test him. She however is attracted to him and comes over to his side. Besides this, a foster-brother reveals the plot (about the girl) to him. Laertes and Fortinbras have been added by Shakespeare.

The original story goes back to the old pre-Christian times and is one of the famous blood-feuds as such are typical of Northern families. In Shakespeare's hands it undergoes a transmutation:

> It is the miracle of Shakespeare's achievement in *Hamlet* that he has transformed such material into a work of enduring and universal appeal.[18]

This change has been possible because of the change brought about in Hamlet's character. In the original story Hamlet is a straightforward character whom the dramatist has changed into his own Hamlet whose well-known complexity has baffled everyone.

There is a play now ascribed to Kyd's (listed as no. 3 above) to which Nashe refers in 1589. From this reference a characteristic of the play emerges: that it was Senecan in nature, such a rhetorical tragedy as *The Murder of Gonzago* is. Henslowe also refers to it in his Diary. It contains a Ghost and the main theme is revenge. This supernatural machinery and revenge-motif both appear in Kyd's *The Spanish Tragedy*, along with the rhetorical style. For these reasons the play has been ascribed to Kyd.

Thus, on the one hand, we have a primitive, pre-Christian revenge tragedy and on the other, we have the polished and sophisticated Hamlet. Pointing out the contrast between them, Kenneth Muir says:

> Shakespeare did not quite succeed in effecting a complete transformation of the old play. He retained incidents and motivations proper to a primitive revenge play, but incompatible with the sophisticated hero of his own.[19]

(d) The Plot of *Hamlet*

The time has now come to cast a glance at the plot of *Hamlet*. First of all, as has been pointed out above, the classical rules of construction had not been observed by Shakespeare. A scene after scene account of the location of the scenes will give an idea of his violation of the unity of place.

Act I

sc. i — A platform outside the castle.

sc. ii — A room of state in the castle.

sc. iii — A room in Polonius's house.

sc. iv — As in the first scene.

sc. v — Another part of the platform.

Act II

sc. i — A room in Polonius's house.

sc. ii — A room in the castle.

Act III

sc. i — A room in the castle.

sc. ii — A hall in the castle.

sc. iii — A room in the castle.

sc. iv — The Queen's closet.

Act IV

sc. i — A room in the castle.

sc. ii — Another room in the castle.

sc. iii — Another room in the castle.

sc. iv — A plain in Denmark.

sc. v — A room in the castle.

sc. vi — Another room in the castle.

sc. vii — Another room in the castle.

Act V

sc. i — Churchyard.

sc. ii — A hall in the castle.

There are, thus, numerous changes in the location of the scenes. The major part of them take place inside the castle, in different rooms, but there are; besides these, three scenes set in the ramparts outside the castle, two in Polonius's house, one in a plain, and one in the churchyard. These frequent changes of scenes defy the unity of place.

The unity of time is also violated in that the play covers the time-span of quite a few months. As Verity observes:

> The events of Hamlet may be supposed to take place in eight days, distributed over a period that may be estimated at about four months.[20]

In the original story, Hamlet goes to England, stays there for a year and then comes back for his revenge. In this play it is not clear how much time has been covered, but, as Verity computes, it is eight months.

The unity of action, the most important of them, has been violated not just once, but quite a few times. Shakespeare has introduced comic scenes into the play to provide contrast and comic relief. The most remarkable of these is the graveyard scene. The scene with Osric is also a comic one. Though these scenes do violate the Aristotelian rules, yet they are important in so far they provide comic relief and contrast. Thus, commenting upon Act I, sc. iii in which Laertes bids farewell to his family Verity says:

> One of the most striking illustrations of Shakespeare's observance of the principle of dramatic relief is the use of scenes that stand out from the main scheme of design and colour, and thereby serve to set it off.[21]

All the three unities, thus, have been violated in the play. His plays are examples of how a work can violate all the rules and yet be a great work of art like *Hamlet*.

It has already been remarked (*Certain Elizabethan Features, supra*) that multiplicity of plots is one of the remarkable features of Elizabethan drama. Hamlet has two plots, the main plot concerning Hamlet and his revenge and the sub-plot concerning Polonius and his family. There are three revenge actions in the play, that are related to Hamlet and Laertes, but both of which are encompassed by the main and the sub-plot. The third revenge action, that concerning Fortinbras, is introduced the first in the play but it cannot be considered as constituting another sub-plot. There are fitul references to Fortinbras throughout the play but he does not influence the action in any way. The Fortinbras plot cannot be considered as a sub-plot, it is but the concluding episode in the play when he comes in to restore the moral order that had been disrupted by the actions of the villain and the hero.

There are, then, two plots in the play. The main plot is concerned with Hamlet whose unconscious jealousy of Claudius is reinforced by the Ghost's revelations. He is instigated by the Ghost to take vengeance upon Claudius and this, after much hesitation and delay, he does take. The main plot contains love-interest in four different ways: (a) the maternal love of Gertrude for Hamlet which is manifested in here very word and action, (b) the filial love of Hamlet for his mother, about which much has been said, including the concept of Oedipus Complex as expounded by Ernest Jones, (c) the friendship between Hamlet and Horatio, and lastly (d) the romantic love between Hamlet and Ophelia which is never manifested on the surface. Actually the fact that Hamlet loved Ophelia is declared only at the end in the graveyard scene. In the play itself, his behaviour towards her is anything but gallant.

The main plot also contains the element of Spectacle (*Opsis*) which is one of the six elements of drama as given by Aristotle. The appearance of the Ghost, the inset play including the Dumb-show, the funeral of Ophelia and lastly the duel are all examples of spectacle. The marching of Fortinbras's Army in Act IV, sc. iv can also be regarded as a spectacle though it is of very short duration. Of these examples of spectacle, the appearances of the Ghost are examples of "the marvellous" as given by Aristotle. Aristotle, of course, says that the marvellous should give pleasure to the audience but here it is the opposite. The Ghost inspires the audience with awe and fear. The inset play supplies the element of spectacle most effectively—the more so because of the effect it has on Claudius. The burial scene is an example of what is termed by Aristotle as "pathetic scenes". The two mad-scenes of Ophelia are also example of pathetic scenes. The duel scene gives martial spectacle which is augmented by the poisoned rapier. This poisoning also affords examples of dramatic irony. In fact both the inset play and the duel scene are masterpieces of spectacle plus dramatic irony, as both of them have purposes other than the superficial one of entertainment—one aimed at exposing the villainy of Claudius and the other aimed at the killing of Hamlet.

Two elements of classical tragedy, *anagnorisis* and *peripeteia* are also present in the main plot. As has been pointed out above (*vide* the discussion of classical rules above) *anagnorisis* is present in the ghost scenes when the Ghost is recognised as the ghost of Hamlet's father. This subtlest kind of *anagnorisis* is presented again and again in the self-revealing soliloquies of Hamlet. Thus, in Act IV, sc. iv, after he has seen Fortinbras prepares to invade Denmark in order to avenge his father's death he analyses himself:

> How stand I then
> That have a father kill'd, a mother stain'd
> Excitements of my reason and my blood,
> And let all sleep.[22]

Such self-revelations are taking place within him throughout the play. Indeed, it is this that has made the play so complex. H.S. Wilson says:

> It is a sign of Hamlet's genius that he can be half-ashamed of the glimpses he catches of himself as he unpacks his heart with words.[23]

Regarding the Queen, she too has a moment of heart-searing self-recognition:

> O Hamlet, speak no more:
> Thou turn'st mine eyes into my very soul;
> And there I see such black and grained spots
> As will not leaves their tinct.[24]

As far as *peripeteia* is concerned, it should be pointed out that M.C. Bradbook has classified the plot of Elizabethan drama into two categories, one is the cumulative plot and the other those with *peripeteia*. She holds that the latter were used in revenge tragedies:

> The plot moves forward in a series of jumps: each small action is ironically constructed.[25]

This is perfectly true of *Hamlet*. Here the episodes that take the action forward have ironic overtones and are separated by scenes and episodes that do not so much contribute to the play as create a mood, an atmosphere, or just afford relief from tension. The action can be said to actually start from sc. v of the first Act in which the Ghost makes his revelations. Immediately afterwards we have a scene that does not contribute an iota to the action as it shows Polonius instructing Reynaldo to spy upon Laertes. After this we have the longest scene in the play in which the action takes a step forward as the performance of *The Murder of Gonzago* is decided upon. The entire play, when analyzed, shows this kind of movement.

But *peripeteia* actually means reversal of fortune, mainly of the hero. Aristotle says:

> Reversal of the Situtation is a change by which the action veer round to its opposite, subject always to our rule of probability or necessity.[26]

This is exactly what happens in the beginning, with the Ghost's revelations. Before that we have Hamlet, very discontented, melancholy, cynical—but he has agreed to stay at Elsinore, giving up the idea of going back to Wittenberg. One can look forward to a settled, courtly life. Then comes the Ghost and he lays the sacred duty of revenge upon him. It changes his whole life, and the change is for the worse, not for the better. This is in accordance with the rule for tragic *peripeteia* as laid down by Aristotle. Thereafter, there is no peace for Hamlet. He pretends to be mad and kills Polonius. He is sent to England after this in disgrace and then comes the final duel with the death of almost everyone concerned including himself. Aristotle's idea of tragedy is perfectly borne out by the main plot of the play and it also shows the characteristics of Elizabethan tragedies as give by Bradbook.

Turning to the sub-plot, we see that it follows the main plot in many particulars. In the main plot there are three characters and so are there in the sub-plot. Here also we have several love-interests: (a) the parental love of Polonius for his two children, (b) the filial love of Laertes and Ophelia for their father, and (c) the sibling love of Laertes and Ophelia. This again is seen on the surface. Ophelia is very gentle and passive and her preferences are not very apparent, but her love for Hamlet does exist as an undercurrent. A.C. Bradley had pointed it out long ago:

> In the Nunnery-scene, Ophelia's first words betray her own feelings...(she) cannot repress the timid attempt to win her lover back by showing that her own heart is unchanged.[27]

The sub-plot has the element of spectacle in only one scene—Ophelia's funeral, and another jointly in the duel-scene. On the other hand, it contains two scenes of pathos. These are the best scenes of Shakespeare and have served as models for many such scenes in later plays. He has also brought in the element of music (one of the six elements of drama) in the songs sung by Ophelia. These songs intensify the element of pathos in the scene.

The element of *anagnorisis* is not present in the sub-plot, but that of *peripeteia* certainly is. Laertes's and Polonius's advice to Ophelia to repulse Hamlet starts the process. Then comes the inadvertent killing of Polonius. This changes everything for Ophelia, she loses her sanity. This real madness parallels Hamlet's feigned madness in the main plot. The pathos of Ophelia's end, however, has no parallel in the main plot, for though the Queen's death is a pathetic one, it cannot compare with that of Ophelia's.

The main plot and the sub-plot of Hamlet are thus related through parallelisms. Almost every event and character in the main plot are paralleled by the sub-plot. There are three characters in both. The revenge action is common to both and reach their end together. The pretended madness of Hamlet is paralleled by the real madness of Ophelia. In their ending again, the two plots are similar, for all the characters die.

Thus, Shakespeare has connected the main plot with the sub-plot through parallelism, but this is not the only way he has brought them together. There is constant interaction between the characters of the main plot and those of the sub-plot. Indeed, there are very few scenes in which the two are not related. There are five scenes in the main plot that have nothing to do with the sub-plot (Act I, scs. i, iv, v, Act IV, scs. iv, vi) and two in the sub-plot (Act I, sc. iii, Act II, sc. i). In ten of the rest of the scenes the characters interact. In three of them (Act IV, scs. i, ii, iii) though the characters of the sub-plot are not physically present yet all three are about Polonius's murder, so in this way, the two plots are related.

A few remarks of eminent critics about the plot should be mentioned. One of the earliest observations in this connection is that of an anonymous critic attributed to be Thomas Hanmer. Remarking on the delay in revenge he most pertinently observes that it is necessary for the play:

> Our Poet, by keeping too close to the Ground-work of his plot, has fallen into an Absurdity.... The Case indeed is this.... Had Hamlet gone naturally to work ...there would have been an End of our play.[28]

This is the most common-sensical and practical solution of the problem of the delay in revenge that has so puzzled the critics. Dr. Johnson has found a grave weakness in the plot in that though there is progress there are many scenes which do not contribute to it. This is perfectly true, as will be seen in a scene-wise analysis of the play (*vide* Ch. V, *supra*).

G. Wilson Knight is of the opinion that the climax of the play occurs in the beginning with the appearance of the Ghost and the rest of the play is but an echo of this resounding beginning:

> The usual procedure is reversed and the climax is at the start. Hamlet, already in despair, converses early with death.[29]

Not many critics will agree with this. Such an opinion is expressed by Knight because he holds that the main theme of the play is death.

There are many more interpretations of the plot, not all of them are acceptable. The very fact that there are so many views about this technical aspect of the play is a pointer to its extreme complexity.

NOTES

1. S.H. Butcher, *op. cit.*, p. 23.
2. Verity, *op. cit.*, p. xxi.
3. Act I, sc. i, ll. 43-44, p. 5.
4. Act II, sc. ii. ll. 526-46, pp. 55-56.
5. T.S. Dorsch, ed and transl., *Classical Literary Criticism*, Penguin Books, 1975, p. 68.
6. *Ibid.*
7. Quoted by Verity, *op. cit.*, p. xxvii.

8. H.S. Wilson, *op. cit.*, pp. 44-45.
9. *Ibid.*, p. 40.
10. Act I, sc. v, ll. 102-03, p. 29.
11. Act II, sc. ii, ll. 582-83, p. 57.
12. Muir, *op. cit.*, p. 79.
13. Act III, sc. ii, ll. 379-80, p. 77.
14. Muir, *op. cit.*, p. 88.
15. Bradbrook, *op. cit.*, p. 45.
16. Verity, *op. cit.*, p. 158.
17. *Ibid.*, pp. xx-xxi.
18. *Ibid.*, p. xlv.
19. Kenneth Muir, *op. cit.*, p. 56.
20. Verity, *op. cit.*, p. xxi.
21. *Ibid.*, p. 147.
22. Act IV, sc. iv, ll. 56-59, p. 96.
23. H.S. Wilson, *op. cit.*, p. 40.
24. Act III, sc. iv, ll. 88-91, p. 84
25. Bradbrook, *op. cit.*, p. 40
26. S.H. Butcher, *op. cit.*, p. 41.
27. Bradley, *op. cit.*, p. 133n.
28. Jump, *op. cit.*, p. 22.
29. Knight, *op. cit.*, p. 42.

9

Imagery in *Hamlet*

Images are word-pictures. They are used in poetry not only to beautify but to render it more effective as well. Images are both functional and decorative, and more. This aspect of Shakespeare's work has been studied pretty exhaustively by modern scholars. The function of his imagery, the relationship between the imagery, the atmosphere and the theme, the development of imagery in his career—all of these have been studied in detail and analysed.

Henri Fluchere has given a very good and acceptable definition of imagery:

> Imagery may shortly defined as a concrete illustration drawn upon by the poet to clarify or embellish the object that he seeks to describe.[1]

Though this definition seems to be quite comprehensive, yet it does not cover Shakespeare's imagery effectively, for his images have many other functions in addition to clarification and embellishment. They illustrate a mood, they foretell future events, they clarify a character's mind, etc.

Often enough, it becomes impossible to distinguish between rhetorical figures, imagery and symbolism in a given work. This is because these features are not only integrally related, but they also overlap. Thus, an image can be studied as a figure of speech if it is expressed accordingly and may also become a symbol, Fluchere has mentioned this characteristic:

> No strict rule allows us to say at what point we pass from the plane of pure psychology, and even the metaphysical plane, in the use of imagery.[2]

Moreover, the same image can easily come under different categories, thus a sense-image will also be a nature image or a domestic image or of any other kind. This is true of all images.

The most obvious and basic categorization is that of sense-images. They correspond to the five senses possessed by human beings. Thus:

Images related to the eye—visual images
Images related to the ear—auditory images
Images related to the nose—olfactory images
Images related to the tongue—gustatory images
Images related to the skin—tactile images

Sense-images may exist independently or may mix and mingle with one other, in which case it will be known as synaesthesia.

As a matter of fact, sense-images can hardly ever stand alone. They usually involve some other aspect of life. They are the most obvious kind of images and *Hamlet* is rich in them. In the examples of images to be given now, most of them shall be taken from the first scene of the first Act for the sake of convenience. When, however, a particular point has to be illustrated, examples will be taken from elsewhere in the play if necessary. The very first image is a visual one:

Bernardo: Have you had quiet guard?
Francisco: Not a mouse stirring.[3]

Here we have a visual image, for a mouse can be seen, but it is also an animal image. This is the case with all sense-images, for they depend upon the fact that an object is being perceived through the senses, so the image will also be related to that particular object. So Horatio's description of the Ghost is a visual image as well as a martial one:

Such was the very armour he had on
When he the ambitious Norway combated;
So frown'd he once when in angry parle,
He smote the sledded Polacks on the ice.[4]

Both of the images here are taken from military prowess and they are both, in addition, visual images as well. Had the image been a little more detailed, for example, if the sound of clanking swords had been mentioned, then the image would have been an auditory one as well.

These two are visual images, but there are images pertaining to other senses as well. Thus Horatio, describing Fortinbras's invasion of Denmark, talks of how he has gathered soldiers to make an army:

> Shark'd up a list of lawless resolutes,
> For food and diet, to some enterprise
> That hath a stomach in't.[5]

Here we have a gustatory image, concerned with eating. Then there are auditory images also. A very fine one is used by Horatio:

> The cock, that is the trumpet to the morn,
> Doth with his lofty and shrill-sounding throat
> Awake the god of day.[6]

This is a very rich image, as it encompasses sense-imagery, animal imagery (cock), musical imagery (trumpet) and religious imagery (god of day). The religious image here refer to Greek religion, but images referring to Christianity are also to be found:

> Wherein our saviour's birth is celebrated,
> The bird of dawning singeth all night long.[7]

Though the original story is set in pre-Christian times, Shakespeare has given it a Christian setting (*vide* Ch. 9, *supra*). This image, too, is a composite one, for here we have auditory image (singeth all night long) along with a religious one.

Different branches of knowledge are used to provide variety. Bernardo, for example, makes use of an image from astronomy:

> When yond same star that's wrested from the pole
> Had made his course to illume that part of heaven
> Where now it burns.[8]

Here the astronomical image of the star is used for the purpose of pointing out the time—thus a concrete image is used to express an abstract idea.

As in the first scene, from which we are taking our examples, there are two officers, it is natural that they should use military images. So, Marcellus uses two martial images in quick succession:

> And why such daily cast of brazen cannon,
> And foreign marts for implements of war.[9]

Horatio, however, is a scholar, so there is variety, in the images he uses. For example, there is an image taken from a branch of knowledge—the law:

> Who, by a seal'd compact,
> Well ratified by law and heraldry,
> Did forfeit, with his life, all those his lands.[10]

Here, along with law, heraldry is also mentioned, so this image carries the double association of law and heraldry. The mention of heraldry is especially relevant because Horatio is talking of a duelling match between the erstwhile king of Norway and the elder Hamlet. In such contests of chivalry heralds played an important part. Such images, taken from different branches of knowledge are to be found throughout the play.

Images from ordinary everyday life are scattered throughout the play, giving it a touch of familiar domesticity. Thus, there are two dress-images in the first scene, both used by Horatio:

> Hath in the skirts of Norway, here and there
> Shark'd up a list of lawless resolutes.[11]

The second image associated with dress is one of the finest images in the whole play:

> But look, the morn, in russet mantle clad
> Walks o'er the dew of yon high eastern hill.[12]

This is an especially effective image because not only is there the colourful visual image of a red mantle, but it also occurs in a personification of morning as a goddess. This would naturally lead to the image of Aurora, the Greek goddess of dawn.

Along with this, there is the image of mountains and of dew—both are images taken from Nature.

An even humbler image taken from ordinary life is that of a labourer, used by Marcellus:

> What might be toward, that this sweaty haste
> Doth make the night joint-labourer with the day?[13]

Here again, abstract and concrete ideas mingle, for the sweaty labourer is something concrete, used to illustrate the abstract idea of haste.

Just as simple, homely images are used in the play, so are elemental, cosmic ones:

> And at his warning
> Whether in sea or fire, in earth or air,
> The extravagant and erring spirit hies.[14]

Here there is reference to just the four elements, the image is not expanded, but a more effective image is also there, which is cosmic in implication:

> Have heaven and earth together demonstrated
> Unto our climatures and countryman.[15]

This is a much grander image than the preceding one, for it encompasses both heaven and earth. Both of these images are taken from the world of nature, though they are not as attractive as the description of dawn given by Horatio.

Just as Shakespeare gives very fine nature-images, so can he give equally awe-inspiring images of supernatural elements. The first scene, as it sets the atmosphere of the play, and prepares us for the appearance of the Ghost, contains many images concerned with supernatural elements. The most horrifying one occurs in Horatio's description of Rome before the assassination of Caesar:

> The graves stood tenantless and the sheeted dead
> Did squeak and gibber in the Roman streets:
> As stars with trains of fire and dews of blood,
> Disasters in the sun.[16]

Here again, we have several images concentrated into one sentence. First of all there are the graves standing empty and the supernatural figures squeaking in the streets. Then there is the stellar image of the unnatural comet with fiery trains and drops of blood raining down from them. The sun, which is always a positive image, is here facing the disaster of eclipse. All these phenomena are supernatural ones and with the bringing in of comets and the sun, get a cosmic and sublime background.

Accumulation of images is one of the remarkable features of Shakespeare's poetry. We have one such instance in Marcellus's speech:

> So nightly toils the subject of the land;
> And why such daily cast of brazen cannon,
> And foreign mart for implements of war;
> Why such impress of shipwrights, whose sore task
> Does not divide the Sunday from the work.[17]

Here we have four images in as many lines: the images of nightly labourers, of cannons, of war instruments and of shipbuilders. This kind of accumulation of images always enhances the effects of descriptions. The lines by Horatio quoted above, "The graves stood tenantless", etc. also give an example of such accumulation, for the list of horrifying events does not end there, but continues for a few more lines, introducing a few more images later.

Shakespeare's images are never just decorative ones, they are functional in many different ways as well. W.H. Clemen has studied the imagery of Shakespeare's plays in detail. This has revealed the important fact that his use of imagery developed with his dramatic art. The images in the early plays serve to beautify the style but as his art matured his imagery has become more and more functional, more and more relevant to the theme, the action and the characters of the play:

> The more Shakespeare becomes a conscious dramatist, the more he employs them for dramatic purposes. The images gradually lose their purely "poetic", often extraneous nature and become one of the dramatic elements.[18]

Analyzing *Hamlet*, he finds a completely new dimension in the images employed by Hamlet himself. This characteristic will be mentioned later, here let us see how the images used by characters other than Hamlet (as in this scene) become functional. For example one of the functions given by Clemen is that of anticipating the future. This scene is indeed an ideal one for this purpose, for it does anticipate the disasters that will overcome the kingdom with the revelations made by the Ghost (*Vide* Ch. *supra*, the analysis of the first scene). Thus when Marcellus describes the appearance of the Ghost for the first time he just employs visual images, not daring to name the Ghost:

Touching this dreaded sight, twice seen of us:
... ...
That if again this apparition come,
He may approve our eyes and speak to it.[19]

These two visual images anticipate the appearance of the Ghost. Later, Horatio's description of supernatural events that occurred before the assassination of Caesar in Rome also anticipate the future bloody events in Denmark itself. They are highly functional and prophetic images, not merely decorative ones.

Besides anticipating the future, Shakespeare's images, instead of being merely decorative, also pass comments on characters and their actions, comments on mankind in general, and carry out many other functions. It has already been observed how Bernardo and Marcellus, being military officers, use martial images and Horatio, being a scholar, has a much wider range of imagery. The martial images used by Marcellus thus highlight his profession, and the images related to chivalry, law, dress, food, classical myths, the elements, the heavenly bodies that have been quoted above, point to the wide knowledge of Horatio.

Not only do the images reveal the profession of the speaker, conversely, Shakespeare chooses his images to suit the personality of the speaker. Thus martial images typify the masculine, strong soldier and delicate, lovely images are employed by Ophelia to suit her delicate personality. There are two female characters in this play and the imagery they use is eloquent of the softness, the elegance of the speaker. Thus, one of the first images used by Ophelia is:

> Himself the primrose path of dalliance treads
> And recks not his own rede.[20]

Another such memorable image, revealing the character of the speaker is used by the Queen in the funeral scene:

> Anon, as patient as the female dove
> When that her golden couplets are disclosed.[21]

Both of these images, as indeed, many others, are indicative of the soft and delicate nature of the two courtly and elegant ladies.

These are some of the images in the first scene (except for the last two), but there are some other kinds of images for which a study of the entire play has to be undertaken. This is not possible here, but a few hints can be given.

What Caroline Spurgeon calls "iterative imagery" helps create the prevailing atmosphere of a play. These are images that recur throughout the play and the whole play has to be studied. About *Hamlet* she remarks:

> (The distinctive atmosphere of *Hamlet*) is partly due to the number of images of sickness, disease, or blemish of the body.[22]

The images of sickness begin with the very first scene when Francisco says:

> For this relief much thanks: 'tis bitter cold
> And I am sick at heart.[23]

Likewise Horatio, trying to think of some reason for the appearance of the Ghost, attributes, it to some kind of ulcer, or tumour, metaphorically, in the kingdom of Denmark:

> But in the gross and scope of my opinion,
> This bodes some strange eruption in our state.[24]

Thus, beginning with the first scene, this iterative image of physical ailments continue throughout the play, creating the impression that, as Marcellus says in a line that has become famous:

> Something is rotten in the state of Denmark.[25]

When accusing his mother of infidelity, Hamlet repeatedly uses words like "sickly" and "apoplexy". In a remarkable image he says:

> It will but skin and film the ulcerous place.
> Whilst rank corruption, mining all within.
> Infects unseen.[26]

He also compares the needless fighting between Norway and Poland to a tumour. Images of disease are strewn throughout his speeches. Spurgeon relates it to the theme of the entire play:

> Thus, to Shakespeare's pictorial imagination, the problem in *Hamlet* is not predominantly that of will and reason...he sees it pictorially, not as the problem of an individual at all, but as...a condition for which the individual is apparently not responsible.[27]

Though most of the examples she gives are from *Hamlet* of the other characters use such images too. Examples have already been given from Francisco and Marcellus, and there is one from Horatio. He attributes the appearance of the Ghost to an "eruption" in our state as quoted earlier.

Iterative images are, thus, extremely functional for they help create the particular atmosphere of the play. The whole play has to be studied.

One of the many important ideas given by Clemen in his analysis of Shakespeare's imagery is that of "imagery-consciousness". Explaining this feature, Clemen says that imagery becomes so much a part of the poet's consciousness that instead of rising to the surface it lies hidden and one has to guess at it:

> The whole image has sunk beneath the surface, as it were, and left behind it only one or two ideas concerned with it. From Shakespeare's middle period on, we are frequently forced to ask what image did Shakespeare have in mind?[28]

There are many such hidden images to be found in the first scene. For example, Horatio says:

But in the gross and scope of my opinion
This bodes some strange eruption to our state.[29]

Here we have the hidden image of a human being.

The image of an ulcer or a tumour is not to be found on the surface. Instead it is a hidden image. Such hidden images are strewn throughout the play. Thus, later, Claudius is speaking to Laertes, asking him to speak without hesitation:

The head is not more native to the heart,
The hand more instrumental to the mouth,
Than is the throne of Denmark to thy father.[30]

Here again, we have the hidden image of a human being. No less than four organs of the body are mentioned, but the basic image of a human being is not mentioned. There is no need to do it either, for the reader has no difficulty in taking in the basic image.

Another term in connection with Shakespeare's imagery as given by Caroline Spurgeon is "image-complex". It is explained thus by Clemen:

> The term "image-complex" is to indicate that Shakespeare in his imagery shows, as Miss Spurgeon has put it, a predilection for "certain classes of things, certain qualities in things and certain aspects of life."[31]

There are many such image-complexes in our poet and Spurgeon cites the examples of imagery concerned with garden and plant-lore. Thus Horatio uses the image-complex of duelling:

Such was the very armour he had on
When he the ambitious Norway combated;
So frown'd he once, when in an angry parle
He smote the sledded Polacks on the ice.[32]

Here there are several images of fighting (one in every line) having to do with the one basic image of single combat. Thus, basically, it is a visual image of military prowess, and also an image-complex involving four short images.

In the above discussion certain aspects of the imagery of *Hamlet* have been mentioned, and, for the sake of convenience the examples, as far as possible, have been taken from only one scene, the first scene of the first Act, in which Hamlet is absent. We shall now have a look at the imagery used by Hamlet himself. This is important, because both Clemen and Spurgeon look at the play from the viewpoint of Hamlet , and how his imagery expounds his character.

There are many valuable ideas Clemen has given in this connection: that his images are all taken from real life, they reveal his "wide educational background", they give relief to conflicting moods, and many more. It is not possible to explain all these ideas here, so only a few of them will be mentioned. Thus in his first soliloquy Hamlet comments on the indecently short interval between the death of his father and the remarriage of his mother, using a homely image:

> A little month, or ere those shoes were old
> With which she follow'd my poor father's body.[33]

Referring to realistic images like these Clemen points out that whereas ordinarily a general thought is expressed through an image, Hamlet uses the opposite method:

> ...he refers the generalization to the events and objects of the reality underlying the thought.[34]

Hamlet's images are connected to his wide knowledge and scholarly life and here Clemen gives a long list of such images. One such evidence of his wide knowledge is to be found in the classical allusions used by him. In the first soliloquy there are two:

> So excellent a king; that was to this,
> Hyperion to a satyr.[35]

Hyperion is the Titan sun-god. The titans reigned in the world before the coming of the Olympian gods. These latter are well-known but the Titans are not so well-known. Hamlet's knowledge of pre-Olympian gods is proof of his scholarship.

Images dealing with conflicting moods, etc. will involve long passages, the most familiar of which is the celebrated soliloquy "To be or not to be". It is a contemplative speech in a serious mood, involving many images. Then comes the Nunnery-scene in which his language undergoes a remarkable change. He makes use of common images: "breeder of sinners", "crawl between heaven and earth", "plague for thy dowry", etc. This change in the language betokens a change in his mood:

> With no other character in Shakespeare do we find this sharp contrast between images marked by a pensive mood and those which unsparingly use vulgar words.[36]

The study of imagery is a very interesting one. Images can be purely ornamental or they can describe actions and thus be functional. They can as in a mature play like *Hamlet*, serve to reflect the mental condition of the speaker. At a higher level, they can relate man to the universe or to God. All these different implications and many others have been studied in detail, throwing light upon Shakespeare's creative processes.

NOTES

1. H. Fluchere, *op. cit.*, p. 167.
2. *Ibid.*
3. Act I, sc. i, l. 10, p. 3.
4. Act I, sc. i, ll. 60-63, pp. 5-6.
5. Act I, sc. i, ll. 98-100, p. 7.
6. Act I, sc. i, ll. 150-52, p. 8.
7. Act I, sc. i, ll. 159-60, p. 9.
8. Act I, sc. i, ll. 36-38, pp. 4-5.
9. Act I, sc. i, ll. 73-74, p. 6.
10. Act I, sc. i, ll. 86-88, p. 6.
11. Act I, sc. i, ll. 97-98, p. 7.
12. Act I, sc. i, ll. 166-67, p. 9.
13. Act I, sc. i, ll. 77-78, p. 6.
14. Act I, sc. i, ll. 152-54, p. 8.
15. Act I, sc. i, ll. 124-25, p. 7.
16. Act I, sc. i, ll. 115-18, p. 7.
17. Act I, sc. i, ll. 72-76, p. 6.
18. W. Clemen, *The Development of Shakespeare's Imagery*, London: Methuen,'77 rpt., p. 81.
19. Act I, sc. i, ll. 25-29, p. 4.

20. Act I, sc. i, ll. 49-50, p. 20.
21. Act V, sc. i, ll. 279-78, p. 122.
22. Caroline Spurgeon, given in Jump, *op. cit.*, p. 41.
23. Act I, sc. i, ll. 8-9, p. 3.
24. Act I, sc. i, ll. 68-69, p. 6.
25. Act I, sc. i, l. 90, p. 14.
26. Act III, sc. iv, ll. 146-48, p. 86.
27. Spurgeon, *op. cit.*, p. 42.
28. Clemen, *op. cit.*, pp. 77-78.
29. Act I, sc. i, ll. 68-69, p. 6.
30. Act I, sc. ii, ll. 47-49, p. 11.
31. Clemen, *op. cit.*, p. 78.
32. Act I, sc. i, ll. 60-63, pp. 5-6.
33. Act I, sc. ii, ll. 147-48, p. 14.
34. Clemen, *op. cit.*, p. 106.
35. Act I, sc. ii, ll. 139-40, p. 14.
36. Clemen, *op. cit.*, p. 109.

10

Poetic Style: Diction and Versification

Shakespeare is known as "the Bard of Avon". This in itself proclaims his poetic achievements. This is an extremely important aspect of our poet's drama and has been studied in detail. Not only does his style reflect his age (that is, it is an Elizabethan-Jacobean style), it reflects his personality as well. Also, the style has to suit each speaker. There are very few dramatists who can fulfill all these requirements.

Elizabethan-Jacobean drama was written in a mixture of prose and verse, and Shakespeare's was no exception to the rule. The characters of the main plot, who are usually noble by birth, speak in verse and the humbler ones in prose. In our play there is a notable exception. Hamlet, when pretending to be mad, and Ophelia when really mad, speak in prose.

It should be borne in mind that poetic style has two clear-cut aspects: diction and versification. In this chapter, both shall be considered separately.

(a) Poetic Diction

There are many classical rules about poetic diction and the Elizabethans were familiar with them. Horace's *Ars Poetica* gives quite clear-cut rules about poetic diction. According to him the diction should vary according to the genre of poetry as well as the character speaking. In drama the characters should speak in conformity with their age, sex and social position, thus:

> It will make a great difference whether a god or a hero is speaking, a man of ripe years or a hot-headed

> youngster in the pride of youth, a woman of standing or an officious nurse, a roving merchant or a prosperous farmer.[1]

This sentence is very comprehensive, for it provides for *dramatis personae* of all kinds. Distinction is made between the divine and the merely human. There are hundreds of varieties among humans and diction must be adjusted to all these. Age and sex must be taken into consideration. Then, according to profession and social status, there are numerous other divisions within these basic categories. Horace points out the difference between a lady and a nurse. He also differentiates between professions, "roving merchant" and "prosperous farmer". These categories can be added to *ad infinitum*. What it all boils down to is that the language must suit the speaker. Diction, thus became highly specialized in later Elizabethan drama. M.C. Bradbrook points out:

> The specific style for princes, for lovers, for clowns, was fixed.[2]

Yet there are certain things that the poet should keep in mind. Not only must the diction be realistic in accordance with the speaker's personality, it must also be such as to persuade the reader or the audience and move him emotionally:

> The Elizabethan dramatist's style is one of impassioned poetic rhetoric, the two commonest functions of which are to persuade and to touch the emotions.[3]

The use of rhetorical figures, as has been pointed out by Aristotle and, subsequently, by other classical rhetoricians, is obligatory. Aristotle thought it important enough to include it in his definition of tragedy when he said that embellishments in proper places is indispensable for poetic diction. Whatever the style might be, grand, or middle or low, figures of speech should be used. Ben Jonson's *The Alchemist* uses characters from a very low social level and, accordingly, he uses the low style. When, however, Sir Epicure Mammon, who belongs to aristocracy, speaks, Jonson easily switches over to the elevated style. But, whoever is speaking, whether it is Face the impostor-cum-servant, or whether it is Sir Epicure, the dramatist uses figures of speech in both of the cases. It is but expected that he should.

In England also, theorists followed the classical masters and recommended the use of rhetorical figures. One of the best-known rhetoricians of the time, George Puttenham, had said in a famous sentence:

> There is nothing so fitte for the poem as to be furnished with all the figures that be Rhetorical and such as do most beautifie the language with eloquence.[4]

Apart from these basics, many other ideas about poetic diction have been expounded by later theorists. Horace's theory of poetic diction is specially well-known. He tells the would-be poet to give a new lease of life to old out-moded words and to use newly-coined words as well. Shakespeare must have been quite familiar with these ideas and had used them to make his style rich and effective.

(b) Diction in *Hamlet*

Shakespeare's dramatic career stretches over quite a long period (*vide* Ch. 3, *supra*), that is, over two decades. Moreover, from the beginning till the end, this is a period of continuous development for him. New territories of dramatic art were conquered as the years passed, so that maturity in years brought maturity in art. His art of characterization and plot-management developed, and along with them his poetic style. Dowden pertinently remarks:

> In point of style the play stands midway between his early and his latest works.[5]

Moreover, he accepts all the conventions of style prevalent in contemporary drama and uses them to serve his own purposes. The use of prose serves not only to distinguish the mad-scenes, whether feigned or real. One of the rules handed down from Aristotle onwards is that the language should be in harmony with the action taking place on the stage. As Aristotle says:

> ...Language enriched in a variety of ways and artistic devices appropriate to the several parts of the play.[6]

In other words, even the same character must not speak in the same manner in different situations. In this play no character illustrates this feature so distinctively as Hamlet. In the soliloquies, in which he is revealing his innermost feelings, he uses a solemn yet informal language. When talking to Horatio he uses the language of ordinary conversation. Yet when speaking to Polonius, Ophelia, Rosencrantz and Guildenstern (when he uses prose) his language is entirely different. There is no formality, yet it is not the friendly way he speaks to Horatio. Then there are the mad-scenes. Ophelia speaks very differently in them from how she speaks to Hamlet in the nunnery-scene, and in her soliloquy on Hamlet ("O what a noble mind", etc.). Claudius, in sc. ii of the first Act speaks in a formal, declamatory manner in the beginning. Then, speaking to Laertes, he changes to the affectionate and informal manner that is expected of him when speaking to the son of a favoured courtier. Some of the stylistic devices used in the play shall now be studied.

(c) Stylistic Devices

Stylistic devices of many kinds are available to a poet. Of them, imagery, symbols and figures of speech are the most common ones. Imagery has already been studied in the foregoing chapter and there are no obvious symbols in *Hamlet*. A few of the most important figures of speech shall now be discussed. As in the case of imagery, some of the figures in Act I, sc ii shall be pointed out.

Similes are the figures of speech most obvious to the reader and this scene contains two remarkable similes. The first one is used by Hamlet to describe his mother. It is a very short one, consisting of half a line only: "Liko Niobe, all tears". This simile, though so short, is effective because of the classical allusion it contains. The other is longer, used by Horatio:

> A figure like your father,
> Armed at point, exactly, cap-a-pe,
> Appears before them, and with solemn march
> Goes slow and stately by them.[7]

This description of the Ghost goes on for few more lines, and can be treated as a Homeric simile.

Right from classical times, metaphors have been given great importance. Shakespeare's metaphors are always remarkable for their great variety and effect. Claudius employs one in describing the relationship between Polonius and himself thus:

> The head is not more native to the heart,
> The hand more instrumental to the mouth,
> Than is the throne of Denmark to thy father.[8]

Here the throne of Denmark or the king, is being compared with a human being. No less than four organs of the human body are mentioned, so it is quite an elaborate metaphor, though it has been given very tersely in just two lines.

Claudius's opening speech is a declamatory one and he uses many figures of speech in it. There are two frozen or hidden metaphors in the first few lines:

> Though yet of Hamlet our dear brother's death
> The memory be green, and that it us befitted
> To bear our hearts in grief, and our whole kingdom
> To be contracted in one brow of woe.[9]

Here there are metaphors of a sapling and of the human face which are submerged in the language, and are not clear-cut, straightforward metaphors.

One of the best-known metaphors in the play occurs in the first soliloquy of Hamlet:

> ...'tis an unweeded garden,
> That grows to seed; things rank and gross in nature.
> Possess it merely.[10]

A garden symbolizes, among other things, man's control over Nature. Here we have a garden where wildness is predominating. It is, therefore, a metaphor that contains a paradox within itself.

Metonymy, a slightly more complex figure, is frequently employed. Thus Claudius says:

> Than is the throne of Denmark to thy father.[11]

Here Shakespeare has substituted the symbol of the throne for the thing symbolized, the king. So the figure used here is a metonymy not a metaphor as in the lines immediately preceding it (quoted above).

Antithesis adds the quality of terseness and pointedness to poetry. Claudius uses quite a few:

With mirth in fun and with dirge in marriage,
In equal scale weighing delight and dole.[12]

Since he is referring to his marriage with Gertrude that followed the funeral of his brother he has to mention both sorrow and happiness and so he uses these antitheses. Hamlet, in a famous line, makes use of one when speaking for the first time:

A little more than kin, and less than kind.[13]

This extremely pithy line contains more than one figure of speech, which will be explained a little later in the discussion on Hamlet's word-play. But besides playing on words Hamlet employs other figures of speech as well. Tautology for example:

'Tis not alone my inky cloak, good mother,
Nor customary suits of Solemn black,
Nor windy suspiration of forced breath,
No, nor the fruitful river in the eye,
Nor the dejected haviour of the visage.[14]

The repetition of the negative has the forced of a declamatory speech. Moreover, here we find the use of litotes also, which is a figure that employs negative words to emphasize a positive fact. Besides these, in the above lines there is onomatopoeia ("windy suspiration of breath") and apostrophe, for the whole passage is addressed to his mother. Thus we have five figures of speech in as many lines: tautology, litote, onomatopoeia, metaphor and apostrophe.

Rhetorical questions add a dramatic quality to poetry and Claudius uses a number of them in this scene when talking to Laertes:

And now, Laertes, what's the news with you?

You told us of some suit; what is't, Laertes?
... ... What wouldst thou beg, Laertes?
That shall not be my offer, not thy asking?
... ...
What wouldst thou have, Laertes?[15]

This entire passage is actually a string of questions. Here there are five questions. Out of these the first four are rhetorical questions and the last an actual one, for Claudius really wants to know what it is that Laertes wants. The mixing of straightforward questions with rhetorical ones makes the passage all the more effective.

Aposeopesis is a figure of speech that works through omission. Hamlet uses many of them in his first soliloquy:

And yet, within a month,
Let me not think on't,—Frailty, thy name is woman!
....
Like Niobe, all tears;—why she, even she—
O God! a beast, that wants discourse of reason,
Would have mourn'd longer—married with my uncle.[16]

Here we have three aposeopeses in the first two lines, and three more in the next three. Hamlet is so perturbed that he breaks off again and again in his speech, leaving his sentences incomplete.

Though he seems to be speaking in a disjointed manner, there is no dearth of figures of speech in this soliloquy-passage. In addition to aposeopesis there are: personification and apostrophe ("Frailty thy name", etc.) Simile ("Like Niobe"), exclamation ("O God!"), hyperbole ("a beast", etc.) and a classical allusion. Yet it does not sound ornamental.

Allusion is a stylistic device often employed by writers to give depth to their poetry. There can be many kinds of allusions, classical, Biblical, topical, etc. In the first soliloquy there are two allusions to classical myths. The first one compares Hamlet's father and his uncle with Hyperion and a satyr respectively:

So excellent a king; that was to this,
Hyperion to a satyr.[17]

He uses the comparison once more in the closet-scene. Indeed, in that speech he makes use of many:

Hyperion's curls, the front of Jove himself;
An eye like Mars, to threaten and commend,
A station like the herald Mercury
New-lighted on the heaven-kissing hill;[18]

Biblical allusions occur very frequently. There is one in the first soliloquy:

Or that the Everlasting had not fix'd
His canon 'gainst self-slaughter.[19]

The reference here is to the Sixth Commandment "Thou shalt not kill" which applies to suicide also. It has been pointed out by Verity that had Shakespeare followed the original story and set the play in pre-Christian times then Hamlet would not have been troubled by such scruples. Claudius, in his turn, has a very effective Biblical allusion:

It hath the primal eldest curse upon't,
A brother's murder![20]

This refers to the story of Cain and Abel. Cain had killed his brother Abel and God had cursed him.

Literary allusions also exist though Shakespeare hardly ever quotes from other works. In *Hamlet* there is mocking reference to literary genres:

...tragedy, comedy, history, pastoral, Pastoral- comical, historical-pastoral, tragical-historiacl, tragical-comical-historical-pastoral, scene individable, or poem unlimited: Seneca cannot be too heavy, nor Plautus too light.[21]

Herein one sentence we have references to literary genres, to scenes, to individual lyrics and to Seneca and Plautus. It is rare indeed to find so many kinds of literary allusions in one sentence. As for direct quotations (which are very rare in Shakespeare) Hamlet uses one:

Come: "the croaking raven doth bellow for revenge."[22]

This quotation is made up from two lines in an old historical play, *The True Tragedie of Richard the Third.* Such direct quotations are very rare. There is one in *As you Like It* in which he not only refers to Marlowe but quotes a line from him.

As has been pointed out earlier in this chapter, poetic style had become extremely compartmentalized in Elizabeathan drama. M.C. Bradbrook has pointed out that the diction for different kinds of characters was expected to be different. Likewise, there were what were known as pattern styles, to be used for different occasions. Bradbrook defines patterned speech thus:

> Patterned speech may be defined as verse which, by an elaborate use of alliteration, assonance, balance of epigrams and clauses, parallelism and repetition or the use of rhetories, stands out from the rest of the play.[23]

One such occasion occurs in the play-within-the-play. Referring to it, Bradbrook observes:

> *The Murder of Gonzago*, like *Pyramus and Thisbe* is written in patterned speech for the same reason; it is on a different dramatic level from the rest of the play.[24]

The style of the inset play thus is different from that of the rest of the play. One of the speeches in it can be taken as an example. It is the speech of the Player Queen which provoked Queen Gertrude to comment "The lady doth protest too much, methinks".[25]

> Nor earth to give me food, nor heaven light!
> Sport and repose lock from me day and night!
> To desperation turn my trust and hope!
> An anchor's cheer in prison be my scope!
> Each opposite that blanks the face of joy,
> Meet what I would have well, and it destroy!
> Both here and hence pursue me lasting strife,
> If once a widow, ever I be wife![26]

The bombastic language of this speech, with its hyperboles, its repetitions and parallelisms, mark it out as a speech patterned after the Senecan plays. The entire inset play is in such a style.

Hamlet's own diction merits special attention as far as irony and word-play is considered. He can hardly speak without quibbles and ambiguities, and puns. A few of them may be mentioned here. His first speech is itself a quibble:

> A little more than kin and less than kind.[27]

This sentence contains anti-thesis, a metaphor and a complex pun. Verity remarks:

> It is significant that Hamlet's first words should be a riddle and cast in that style of ironic jesting which he uses so effectively.[28]

Here the word "Kin" means cousin and "Kind" means (a) son, (b) species, and (c) the sentiment of leniency. So many levels of meaning along with other figures make the sentence more of a riddle than anything else. His next sentence is:

> Not so, my lord; I am too much i'the sun.[29]

It contains the metaphor of the sun which is a continuation of the same metaphor in the previous sentence, but it has been used by Hamlet to mean several things. It is a pun on the word "son" and that word has several implications. On the surface the sun will mean the king, that is, Hamlet says that he is too much in the favour of the king. He also means that he is in much too intimate a relationship to the king for he is (a) son to his father, the elder Hamlet, (b) son to a mother who has turned to an incestuous relationship, and (c) son and nephew to his uncle-father Claudius. Nearly all of his sayings and word-play have this kind of complexity. D.G. James, for example, finds riddles at many levels in the play: riddle of character, riddle of the player's art, riddle of action, etc.

(d) Versification

Diction and versification are but two sides of the same coin of poetic style. No discussion of a poet's style can be complete unless both of these are dealt with. Prosody, however, is an extremely technical aspect of poetry and needs special training. Henri Fluchere has pointed out:

> It is by its rhythm as much as by its images that a verse is expressive. The rhythmical succession has an emotional pattern, shows a purpose, imposing a mood or defining a thought.[30]

Blank verse is the poetic form used in Elizabethan drama. This means a passage of unrhymed iambic pentametres. The iambic metre comprises two syllables, of which the first is unstressed and the second is stressed. Each line contains five such feet. A few lines from Claudius's first speech are given below as an example of regular blank verse:

> Now foll/ows, that/you know,/young For/tinbras,/
> Holding/a weak/suppop/sal of/our worth,/
> Or think/ing by/our late/dear broth/er's death/
> Our state/to be/disjoint/and out/of frame.[31]

This is a passage of four lines, has no rhymes and all the lines are iambic pentametres. Passages of such perfectly regular blank verse are quite rare, for usually one or two feet of other metres also occur. Such irregularities do but enhance the flexibility of a passage of blank verse and are desirable features.

Versification has many complexities. There can be end-stopped lines or run-on ones. The former is the kind of line that requires the reader to make a definite pause at the end. If the reader (or the actor), has to stop at the end of every line then that makes the verse sound artificial and jerky instead of natural and smooth. Early Elizabethan plays often give such passages. The inset play, in which Shakespeare has mocked such plays, gives many good examples of end-stopped passages. But Shakespeare, often, made deliberate use of end-stopped lines in order to produce a certain effect:

> Yet so far hath discretion fought with nature,
> That we with wisest sorrow think on him,
> Together with remembrance of ourseleves.
> Therefore our sometime sister, now our queen,

The imperial jointress to this warlike state,
Have we, as 'twere with a defeated joy.[32]

Here Shakespeare has deliberately used end-stopped lines in order to heavily stress each of the lines. Each line is like a hammer-blow and is very effective since it is a formal, declamatory speech.

The opposite of these is the run-on line, also known as enjambements. No punctuation mark is given at the end of the lines, so the lines flow smoothly into each other. The majority of good blank verse are of this type. Claudius's first speech begins in this manner:

Though yet of Hamlet, our dear brother's death
The memory be green, and that it us befitted
To bear our hearts in grief, and our whole kingdom
To be contracted in one brow of woe.[33]

The actor, while declaiming these lines, does not have to pause at the end. Instead he can move on to the next, pausing where he pleases to take breath. This gives a natural flow to the lines.

While declaiming the lines, a short, almost infinitesimal pause often has to be made within the line. This is known as the caesura or the medial pause. Mediaeval narrative poetry had a special feature from this point of view. It had a well-marked pause in the middle of the line, as can be seen in the poetry of Langland and others. This, along with the end-stopped feature, gave the verse a jerky, mechanical quality. The Elizabethan dramatists did away with this custom and varied the positioning of the caesura from line to line:

Upon a fearful summons // I have heard
The cock, // that is the trumpet to the morn,
Doth with his lofty // and shrill sounding throat,
Awake the god of day; // and at his warning.[34]

Here the first contains one caesura after the seventh syllable, but in the second the caesura falls after the second. Again in the third line the caesura falls after the fifth syllable and in the fourth after the sixth. Thus the actor shall pause at different times to take breath. This will lead to smoothness and also give a conversational quality to the lines.

Often enough, for special effect, the writer may give more than one caesura in the same line. Thus in the lines given below there are more than just one caesurae for special purposes:

> She married // O, // most wicked speed!
> It is not, // nor it cannot come to, // good:
> But break, // my heart, // for I must hold my tongue![35]

Here Hamlet, from whose first soliloquy these lines are taken, is in a very disturbed condition. He speaks in a disjointed manner, often pausing for breath. So the lines have more than one caesurae. This is true of most of the lines in this soliloquy.

By definition (iambic pentametres) blank verse lines should contain ten syllables. But, in order to give flexibility to their poetry poets often vary the length of their lines:

> 'Tis gone, and will not answer.[36]

This line contains only seven syllables instead of ten whereas the following has twelve of them:

> Let me not think on't,—Frailty, thy name is woman![37]

Another way of introducing variety in blank verse is the use of stichomythia. This can be of many kinds. An intricate variety of this can be seen when the one and the same line is broken up between different speakers:

> *Horatio*: Do, if it will not stand.
> *Bernardo*: 'Tis here!
> *Horatio*: 'Tis here![38]

This line has been broken up twice, that is, it is spoken in three divisions, yet it is a pentametre.

Apart from blank verse, which is unrhymed, rhymed couplets are also used in these plays. First of all there are the Senecan couplets that point out a moral, sum up the theme, or highlight a mood. Both of the last two are to be seen in the famous couplet:

> The time is out of joint: O cursed spite,
> That ever I was born to set it right![39]

But apart from such couplets, the characters also at times speak in rhymed couplets. Such speeches, isolated as they are from the body of the play because of their rhymes, often carry a special atmosphere and a special meaning. One such passage occurs in the graveyard scene:

> Imperial Caesar, dead and turn'd to clay,
> Might stop a hole, to keep the wind away:
> O, that that earth which kept the world in awe
> Should patch a hole to expel the winter's flaw![40]

The most remarkable use of couplets in Hamlet, of course, occurs in *The Murder of Gonzago*. The entire play, or as much of it as is seen, is in heroic couplets. The Player King begins it:

> Full thrity times hath Phoebus' cart gone round
> Neptune's salt wash and Tellus' orbed ground,
> And thrity dozen moons with borrow'd sheen
> About the world have times twelve thirties been,
> Since love our hearts, and Hymen did our hands,
> Unite communal in most sacred bands.[41]

Apart from blank verse, there are also songs in the play. *Hamlet* contains songs that are snatches of well-known ballads. There are three of them sung by Ophelia in her madness and one sung by the first Grave-digger in the graveyard scene. Ophelia's songs are intensely pathetic as they have to do with death and love and have inspired other mad scenes by other dramatists. It should be noted here that in the text being used Verity the editor has omitted twelve lines in the song "To-morrow is St. Valentine's day". Perhaps this is because these later stanzas contain some indecent lines, usually referred to as "Ophelia's bawdy songs". The Grave-digger's song is a comic one, throwing into relief the macabre nature of his work.

As this very brief account shows, music, both vocal and instrumental, often plays a very important part in Shakespeare's plays. Hamlet, though a mature work, is still a comparatively early play and in it music does not have the significance that if has, for example, in *The Tempest*. Aristotle, as a matter of fact, counts music as one of the six elements of drama and therefore the Elizabethans included songs in their plays. Such songs abound in comedies, but are fewer in number in tragedies. In *Hamlet* Ophelia's songs serve to make the scene highly pathetic and the Grave-digger songs serve both as comic relief and as contrast.

The different aspects of poetic style, as have been sketchily dealt with, form one facet of the play. In this chapter almost all the examples of figures of speech have been taken from one scene only, Act I, sc. ii, just as in the preceding chapter most of the images had been taken, for the sake of convenience, from Act I, sc. i. The earnest student will realise what variety and wealth of imagery and rhetoric can be found in the rest of the play.

NOTES

1. T.S. Dorsch, *op. cit.*, p. 83.
2. Bradbrook, *op. cit.*, p. 45.
3. H. Fluchere, *op. cit.*, p. 152.
4. Quoted by Fluchere, *op. cit.*, p. 159.
5. Jump, *op. cit.*, p. 35.
6. T.S. Dorsch, *op. cit.*, p. 39.
7. Act I, sc. ii, ll. 198-201, p. 16.
8. Act I, sc. ii, ll. 47-49, p. 11.
9. Act I, sc. ii, ll. 1-4, p. 9.
10. Act I, sc. ii, ll. 135-37, p. 14.
11. Act I, sc. ii, l. 49, p. 11.
12. Act I, sc. ii, ll. 12-13, p. 10.
13. Act I, sc. ii, l. 65, p. 11.
14. Act I, sc. ii, ll. 77-81, p. 12.
15. Act I, sc. ii, ll. 42-50, p. 11.
16. Act I, sc. ii, ll. 145-51, p. 14.
17. Act I, sc. ii, ll. 139-40, p. 14.
18. Act III, sc. iv, ll. 56-59, p. 83.
19. Act I, sc. ii, ll. 131-32, p. 13.
20. Act III, sc. ii, ll. 37-38, p. 79.
21. Act II, sc. ii, ll. 380-84, p. 51.
22. Act III, sc. ii, ll. 239-40, p. 73.
23. Bradbrook, *op. cit.*, p. 97.

24. *Ibid.*, p. 103.
25. Act III, sc. ii, l. 219, p. 72.
26. Act III, sc. ii, ll. 205-12, p. 72.
27. Act I, sc. ii, l. 65, p. 11.
28. Verity, *op. cit.*, p. 143.
29. Act I, sc. ii, l. 67, p. 11.
30. H. Fluchere, *op. cit.*, p. 181.
31. Act I, sc. ii, ll. 17-20, p. 10.
32. Act I, sc. ii, ll. 5-10, p. 10.
33. Act I, sc. ii, ll. 1-4, pp. 9-10.
34. Act I, sc. i, ll. 149-52, p. 8.
35. Act I, sc. ii, ll. 165-68, p. 14.
36. Act I, sc. i, l. 52, p. 5.
37. Act I, sc. ii, l. 146, p. 14.
38. Act I, sc. i, l. 141, p. 8.
39. Act I, sc. v, ll. 189-90, p. 33.
40. Act V, sc. i, ll. 206-9, p. 119.
41. Act III, sc. ii, ll. 144-49, p. 70.

11

Critical Reception of *Hamlet*

From the very beginning, *Hamlet* has been a highly popular play on the stage. The chief reason for its popularity among contemporaries was the fact that it was a revenge tragedy with that very popular figure, a "melancholy man" as its hero. After that, especially from the nineteenth century onwards it is the play itself that gained prominence. This is not peculiar to the twentieth century alone for Coleridge had declared that he had "a smack of Hamlet" himself. The tendency continued well into late twentieth century. Thus, Harry Levin had said:

> (Hamlet's) circumstances are ours to the extent that every man, in some measure, is born to privilege and anxiety, committed where he has never been consulted, hemmed in on all sides by an overbearing situation, and called upon to perform what must seem an ungrateful task.[1]

There is an opinion that *Hamlet* should not be acted, that its impact is lessened if it is put on the stage. Many nineteenth century critics were of this opinion. Hazlitt had declared:

> We do not like to see our author's plays acted, least of all *Hamlet*. There is no play that suffers so much in being transferred to the stage.[2]

Yet the play's popularity on the stage did not suffer any eclipse. By the middle of the nineteenth century G.H. Lewes had declared:

> Performed in barns and minor theatres than in Theatres Royal, it is always and everywhere attractive.[3]

More experiments have been carried out with *Hamlet* than with any other play, particularly in the twentieth century. It is a well-known fact that *Hamlet* is the longest play of Shakespeare. The full play is so long that it cannot be performed in less than six hours if the play is put up without any cuts. So each director selects and cuts according to his own convenience. Jan Kott observes:

> One can perform only one of several Hamlets potentially existing in this arch-play.[4]

It is this fact, together with the character of the hero, that has given rise to many interpretations of the play, not only in criticism but in stage-performances as well. It has been produced as a play of the Renaissance with period costumes. Going to the other extreme it has been performed as a mediaeval play in mediaeval armour on one hand and in modern evening dress on the other. A brief account of some of the outstanding performances of the twentieth century will now be given.

A French version of *Hamlet* named *Le Mariage d' Hamlet* was produced in 1922 by Jean Sarment. It opens seventeen years after the death of Hamlet, in Heaven. Polonius, Hamlet and Ophelia want a second chance to prove how differently they would live their lives if they had another chance to do so. God grants them the chance and they are born with unimpaired memories. They are born in a middle-class family and the play proceeds with a lot of misunderstandings and accidents, till they all die. This Hamlet is a bourgeois Hamlet, pining for recognition as a royal person.

In 1930 the father of German Naturalist drama, Gerhart Hauptmann, produced *Hamlet* in Wittenberg—a play written in the Elizabethan mode of a five-act tragedy in blank verse, but he changed the plot. The character of Hamlet resembles the original in that he is melancholy almost to madness. The play is set in the mediaeval times at the University of Wittenberg. It ends, not with death of Hamlet, but with the declaration that King Hamlet of Denmark is dead and therefore the student Hamlet (who is the hero) is heir to the throne. It is also imputed that he will never ascend the throne.

An American version of the play was produced in 1949, written by Percy Mackaye. It is composed like Elizabethan plays, in a mixture of verse and prose but it differs most significantly from them in that it is a tetralogy entitled *The Mystery of Hamlet, King of Denmark*. In brief, the first of these plays, *The Ghost of Elsinore*, contains the murder of Yorick's daughter by Claudius who had actually meant to kill infant prince Hamlet. The second play is named *The Fool in Eden* and is concerned with Claudius's villainy who murders Yorick because he knows too much. Hamlet is seven years old in this play. The third is *Odin Against Christus* and gives the situation twenty years later in which King Hamlet goes mad. The fourth play *The Serpent in the Orchard* depicts the murder of king Hamlet by Claudius. In other words the writer presents imaginary situations before Shakespeare's *Hamlet* starts.

Bern Kops produced an English *Hamlet* in 1956 named *The Hamlet of Stepney Green*. This is a fully realistic play, set amongst the Jewish immigrants in London's East End. It is in prose and David, the Hamlet of the play, gets married to the girl next door and the Ghost blesses the married couple.

It was in the same year also that at Cracow *Hamlet* was produces as a drama of political criticism. Everyone in the play undergoes a political interpretation:

> "To be" means for him to revenge his father and to assassinate the king; whereas "not to be" means to give up the fight.[5]

The realistic interpretation is also to be found in *Return to Dane's Hill*, performed in 1958 by Ashley Dukes. It is a three-act "tragic comedy". The time is the present time and the setting is an English country house. At the end of the play Andrew (Hamlet) who is a scientist leaves his home Dane's Hill, for he comes to know that his father knew of a long-standing affair between his wife and his brother.

Cue for Passion, produced in 1958 was an expressionistic play produced in America by Elmer Rice. It is a play containing five scenes, set in a country house.

Besides these there have been many productions of the play. Goethe's *Wilhelm Meister Lehrjahre* became famous and he, not being content with having produced a play, later wrote a novel. Indeed, many works of fiction have been influenced by *Hamlet*. In the field of drama, the influence continues well into the twentieth century and beyond. Pirandello's *Henry IV* in its plot resembles *Hamlet*. Brecht had prepared a radio broadcast of it. Tom Stoppard's *Rosencrantz and Guildenstern Are Dead* is a highly influential modern adaptation.

In the world of literacy criticism also, it has been acclaimed as one of his best plays, if not the best. It was in the eighteenth century that Hamlet's character started to gain importance, Particularly because of Garrick's interpretation of him as a sensitive and melancholy man. The flaw of procrastination was first recognised by Hanmer in the eighteenth century who justified the delay in action as being one of the exigencies of the play. By the second half of the century Dr. Johnson's analysis of the play became available. In it he gives succinct remarks on different features of the play. Apart from observations on the different elements of the play like the pretended madness of the hero and the real one of the heroine, the plot, the character of Hamlet, he makes, in his own way, a very perceptive remark:

> The plot is accused of having shown little regard to poetical justice and may be charged with equal neglect of poetic probability.[6]

He makes this remark in connection with the Ghost's enjoining upon Hamlet the duty of avenging him. According to him it is not very probable.

Interpretation of the character of Hamlet eclipsed all the other features of the play from the nineteenth century onwards. Hazlitt, Lamb, Coleridge, everyone interpreted it in a different manner. Lamb found him to be a "shy, negligent, retiring" young man. Coleridge described him as a person of massive intellect and Hazlitt as "the most amiable of misanthropes." The late nineteenth century became aware of the special symbolic status of Hamlet. The way to understand Shakespeare, for these critics, was through character-analysis and

A.C. Bradley's work is the best product of the approach (*vide* Ch. VII, the character of Hamlet).

In the twentieth century, more complexity was added to the critical approaches to *Hamlet*. First of all, different critical theories were used to read the plays. Ernest Jones's *Hamlet and Oedipus* uses the psychoanalytical approach to *Hamlet*, interpreting the actions and motives of the character from this point of view. One of the results of this approach is the opinion that Hamlet unconsciously identifies himself with Claudius:

> The call of duty to kill his step-father cannot be observed because it links itself with unconscious call of his nature to kill his mother's husband, whether this is the first or the second.[7]

Apart from the analysis of individual characters, particularly that of the hero, other kinds of studies were also done. Geoffrey Bullough made a thorough research into the sources of Shakespeare's plays, published under the title of *Narrative and Dramatic Sources of Shakespeare*. Many critics studied his plays against the Elizabethan philosophical view of the cosmos, particularly Theodore Spencer and Lily B. Campbell. His imagery was studied in detail by Caroline Spurgeon and Wolfgang Clemen as has been mentioned in Ch. 10, *supra*. Interest was revived in Elizabethan stage conventions by M.C. Bradbrook's *Themes and Conventions in Elizabethan Tragedies* and studies were made accordingly.

Of late, especially after the Second World War, his plays are being studied from the points of view of different critical theories: structuralism, post structuralism, narratology, etc. All yield fruitful results, casting new lights upon his plays. The feminist theory, for example, concentrates on Gertrude and looks at the play from a different angle. Rebecca smith vindicates her of the charges of adultery and of taking part in the murder of her husband. The same is the case with Lisa Jardine's analysis of Gertrude's character. Instead of looking at her as a lecherous and murderous woman she looks upon her as the victim of Hamlet's thwarted ambition. Jardine looks into the future and says that if Hamlet remained childless it will be the son of Claudius and Gertrude who will become the king and this makes Hamlet even more bitter.

The diligent student will realise that all such interpretations are possible and partially valid. Nothing exhausts the possibilities in Shakespeare because of the complexity of the plays.

NOTES

1. Harry Levin, *The Question of Hamlet*, quoted in Ruby Cohn, *Modern Shakespearean Offshoots*, New Jersey: Princeton University Press, 1976, p. 107.
2. Jump, *op.cit.* p. 29.
3. *Ibid.*, p. 33.
4. *Ibid.*, p. 196.
5. *Ibid.*, p. 200.
6. *Ibid.*, p. 24.
7. Ernest Jones, *Hamlet and Oedipus* in Jump., *op.cit.*, p. 61.

Some Important Questions

1. "Hamlet, in spirit and intention, does not avenge his father, he avenges himself." Elucidate.
2. "Hamlet is not the sole avenger of the play." Who are the others and how do they influence the plot?
3. "The real subject of the play is the effect of a mother's guilt on a son." Do you agree? Give reasons for your answer with reference to the text.
4. "The ghost arouses our pity; as it does Hamlet's." Elucidate with special reference to the text.
5. Give a critical account of the closet-scene.
6. Write a critical analysis of the nunnery-scene.
7. Examine Hamlet as a revenge tragedy.
8. "Of the feigned madness of Hamlet, there appears no adequate cause, for he does nothing which he might not have done with the reputation of sanity." Comment.
9. "The appearance of the ghost in *Hamlet* is a master-stroke of its kind." Elucidate with special reference to the text.
10. Give a character analysis of Hamlet.
11. "Hamlet (the man) is dominated by an emotion which is inexpressible, because it is in excess of the facts as they appear." Do you agree?
12. "The soliloquies of Hamlet are excellent example of the slow, dwelling verse which Shakespeare appropriates to the utterance of thought in solitude." Elucidate.

Select Bibliography

Bayley, John, *Shakespeare and Tragedy*, Routledge and Kegan Paul, London, 1981.

Bradbrook, M.C., *Themes and Conventions of Shakespearean Tragedy*, Cambridge University Press, 1935.

Bradley, A.C., *Shakespearean Tragedy*, London: Routledge, 1960.

Bratchell, D.F. (ed.), *Shakespearean Tragedy*, London: Routledge, 1990.

Campbell, Lily B., *Shakespeare's Tragic Heroes*, Cambridge University Press, 1930.

Clemen, W., *The Development of Shakespeare's Imagery*, London: Methuen, 1951.

Evans, B., *Shakespeare's Tragic Practice*, Oxford University Press, 1978.

Jump, John (ed.) *Hamlet: A Casebook*, Hound Mills, Palgrave, 1968.

Knight, G. Wilson, *The Wheel of Fire*, Oxford University Press, 1938.

Lawlor, John, *The Tragic Sense in Shakespeare*, London: Chatto and Windus, 1960.

Leech, Clifford, *Shakespeare's Tragedies*, London: Chatto and Windus, 1950.

Levin, Harry, *The Question of Hamlet*, Oxford University Press, 1959.

Madariaga, Salvador de, *On Hamlet*, Hollis and Carter, 1948.

Nicoll, Allardyce (ed), *Shakespeare Survey 9*, Cambridge University Press, 1956.

Williamson, C.C.H. (ed), *Readings on the Character of Hamlet*, London: Allen and Unwin, 1950.

Index